One Way
to
Play Football

Al Janssen
and
21 NFL Stars

Illustrations
by Phillip Gianopulos

CROSS ROADS BOOKS
Atlanta, Georgia

Library of Congress Cataloging in Publication Data
Main entry under title:
Pro Athletes Outreach
  One Way to Play Football

   1. Football-Addresses, essays, lectures.   2. Football players--United
States--Biography--Addresses, essays, lectures.   I. Janssen, Al.
ISBN 0-89989-024-5

Dedication

I would like to dedicate this book to my parents, who have continually encouraged me in all of my writing projects; and to Pro Athletes Outreach, who have provided spiritual assistance for most of the players in this book, and many other players in the National Football League.

Table of Contents

Preface

A book such as "One Way to Play Football" needs a disclaimer. In no way is this to be considered the ultimate treatise on football. The twenty-one professional football players who have contributed to this book are giving a few of the basic techniques and principles that have made them successful. It is impossible for them, in the space of a few pages, to detail every move they make, every technique they use, and every situation they face during the course of a single football game.

The purpose of this book is three-fold. For beginners in the game of football, it will teach them the basics. For young ball players in this category, it would be wise for them to read the entire book in order to gain a good head knowledge about each position and technique. A good football player is one who uses all of the basic skills. While a linebacker rarely handles the football, for example, he should still know how to run with the ball when the opportunity presents itself through an interception or fumble recovery. Also, he should understand how quarterbacks, running backs and offensive linemen think so he can more effectively defend against them.

The second purpose of this book is to provide some tips for older football players. These pros are among the best at their positions and have spent years perfecting their skills. They have attempted to pass some of this knowledge on to you, to help you polish your skills.

Finally, and most important, these pros have a message to communicate. Part of it concerns the attitudes that make them successful football players—their discipline, their motivation, their determination. But even more than that, it goes to the root of success in any endeavor, whether it be football or any field.

Some of these attitudes are communicated in each chapter. But also, each player has summarized his beliefs in a personalized message in chapter twenty-one. Then in the final chapter, one of the top offensive linemen in the NFL, Norm Evans, explains how to build this foundation in your life. It is the starting point, rather than the conclusion, for this book.

There are several people I would like to thank for their help in preparing this manuscript. First, to the football players and staff involved with Pro Athletes Outreach (PAO)—for their leads and encouragement. PAO, a Christian training program for competing pro athletes, was started by several of the football players in this book.

Second, thanks is due to the public relations departments of various NFL teams who provided biographical information, pictures, and on occasion helped line up the interviews. Third, to Diana Collings and Dorothy Forrest who typed the manuscript.

And a special thanks to Gene Foster. Gene was technical advisor throughout the project, helping to mesh the various techniques and terminology from more than twenty different ball players into one consistent package. A couple of words on Foster's background. Gene played ten years of professional football as a running back, six of those with the San Diego Chargers. He now heads the Gene Foster Instructional Football School in Tempe, Arizona, which provides outstanding instruction for football players of all ages.

--Al Janssen

HISTORY

On a chilly November afternoon in 1823, a soccer match was reaching its 5:00 conclusion as the ball began to descend toward William Webb Ellis of the Rugby Boys School in England. Perhaps frustrated with the impending tie or displeased with his soccer skills, Ellis shocked his mates by catching the ball rather than heading it or kicking it. He then cradled the ball close and charged across the goal line as the 5:00 bell rang.

Ellis was much criticized for his shocking behavior, but his impulse led to the formation of a new sport in England—rugby—which became the forerunner of the American game known as football. The first recognized football game in the United States was played between Princeton and Rutgers on November 6, 1869. Actually a primitive form of soccer, its only resemblance to the modern game was that players were allowed to run interference when a teammate possessed the ball. Rutgers won that first match by a score of 6 to 4.

In 1873, five "Ivy League" schools organized the first meeting to establish uniform rules for a soccer-like game they called football. But the significance of that meeting was in the school that decided not to attend. Princeton, Rutgers, Columbia and Yale agreed upon rules that resemble what we call soccer, but Harvard boycotted the meeting in favor of what they called the "Boston Game," a game much closer to present-day football. If they hadn't, soccer might well be the number one sport in the U.S. today.

Looking for a new opponent to play their game, Harvard invited a Canadian school, McGill, to play a two-game series in May of 1874. One game was played under the Boston rules, the second under McGill's Canadian rugby rules, which allowed a player to pick up the ball and run with it at any time. The spectators and Harvard players

11

immediately took to the game. The next year, Harvard converted its arch rival, Yale, and the two schools played the first game of a series that has produced some of the keenest rivalry in college football. Other schools quickly teamed up for this exciting sport.

In those days, when a player carried the ball over the goal line, no points were scored. A touchdown simply awarded a team a free kick. In subsequent years, the touchdown gained increasing importance until it equalled and then surpassed the value of a successful kick.

As the game moved into the 1880's, it remained essentially a rugby-like game since the ball was kicked and carried freely with little attempt at strategy. Walter Camp, the man credited with being the father of American football, inserted some order into the game by introducing the idea of scrimmage. Rather than dropping the ball between two teams who would fight for possession, Camp gave the ball to one team and they planned offensive strategy, while their opponents attempted to stop them. After a score, the teams exchanged control of the ball. That idea won acceptance until the Yale-Princeton game of 1881 in which each side held the ball for an entire half while scoring no points; each believed that a draw would give them claim to the "national" championship. Camp then suggested a series of downs, giving each team three chances to either gain five yards or lose 10 yards. The loss provision later faded and, within a few years, the rules we know today of four "downs" to gain 10 yards became accepted. Camp also helped establish the limit of 11 players to a side and originated the first all-American teams.

As football moved from the 1880's to 90's, college ball became very popular and spread to local athletic clubs where players could continue to compete after their collegiate career. The first football player to admit accepting money did so in 1892 while playing for the Allegheny Athletic Club. He was William "Pudge" Heffelfinger, a former star at Yale, and Allegheny paid him $500 to play against the Pittsburgh Athletic Club. "Pudge" scored the only touchdown (then worth four points) to lead his team to a 4-0 win. Other clubs soon followed the Allegheny example and began paying players. One such club, the Morgan Athletic Club, was founded in 1898, later became the Chicago Normals, then the Racine Cardinals, Chicago Cardinals, and today is known as the St. Louis Cardinals. It is the oldest continuing operation in professional football.

A forerunner of the National Football League existed briefly in 1902 when a team, led by famous baseball manager Connie Mack, claimed the first pro championship. Still the colleges dominated public attention, especially those teams centered on the northeastern seaboard. Michigan was the first midwest team to attract attention with a powerful "point a minute" squad that won the first Rose Bowl game over Stanford 49-0 in 1902. The granddaddy of all bowl games took a 14 year break after the rout.

The next significant innovation in football was the forward pass which was first introduced into the rules in 1905 at a special meeting headed, again, by Walter Camp. The meeting was organized after President Theodore Roosevelt, alarmed by the increasing number of deaths and serious injuries, threatened to ban the game if the rules were not changed to make it safer. Rules laid down at this meeting established a neutral zone at the line of scrimmage, limited mass interference, and increased the first-down yardage requirement from five yards in three tries to ten yards. In the next six years, other changes were made requiring seven men on the offensive line, dividing games into 15 minute quarters, lengthening the field set at 100 yards by adding 10-yard endzones for catching forward passes, introducing a fourth down, and establishing the present scoring system.

Necessary as those changes were, it was the rules permitting the forward pass that propelled football into the modern era. Since the ball in the early 1900's was shaped more for kicking than passing, few teams took immediate advantage of the new rules. It wasn't until 1913, when Notre Dame shocked Army 35-13 by using passes from

Gus Dorais to Knute Rockne, that the forward pass became a serious weapon in football.

The great football heroes of this era were Jim Thorpe and his team, the Carlisle Indians, coached by "Pop" Warner. The Carlisle team rarely had more than three substitutes available for a game, yet the tiny school played the best teams in college football and consistently defeated them. Thorpe and his teammates were all-around players. Besides being a great runner, Jim played rough defense and was the team's top kicker. After starring in the 1912 Olympics, Thorpe played professional baseball and spent several seasons in pro football. In 1916, he helped the Canton Bulldogs win 10 straight games, leading to their claim as the champions of the world. Thorpe was chosen president of the American Professional Football Association, which later evolved into the National Football League, in 1920.

But pro football didn't capture the public eye until Red Grange, the super star from Illinois, joined the league in 1925. Nicknamed "The Galloping Ghost," Grange is considered one of the greatest football players of all time. In 1924, in a game against Michigan, the Illinois halfback helped dedicate his school's new stadium by scoring four touchdowns on four carries during the first 12 minutes of the game. His runs covered 95, 67, 56 and 44 yards. Although played sparingly the rest of the game, Grange scored one more touchdown and passed for a sixth in what many consider the greatest single performance in college football history.

After the 1925 college season, Grange signed a contract with the Chicago Bears and 38,000 people watched him play in the traditional Thanksgiving Day game against the Cardinals. The Bears and Grange then embarked on a barnstorming tour, playing seven games in 11 days. The highlight was a game in New York when a record 70,000 fans turned out to see the Bears play the Giants, thus helping to establish pro football in the nation's largest city.

But the nation's football mania still concentrated primarily on the universities. This was the era of legends:

the Four Horsemen of Notre Dame and their great coach Knute Rockne; "Wrong Way" Roy Riegels, the man who cost his team the Rose Bowl in 1929 by carrying a fumble 60 yards in the wrong direction (many still claim it is the most famous single play in football history); and great individual stars like Bronko Nagurski and Ernie Nevers and coaches such as Amos Alonzo Stagg and Fielding Yost.

The 1930's heralded the birth of three new post-season games to rival the Rose Bowl. The Orange, Cotton and Sugar Bowls are still the leaders among the numerous post-season contests that now compete for attention during the Christmas and New Year holiday seasons each year.

In 1935, the Heisman Trophy was inaugurated. Named after John Heisman, the great coach from Georgia Tech, the award honors the outstanding college football player in America. Presented each year by the Downtown Athletic Club of New York, its first winner was Jay Berwanger, a halfback for the University of Chicago. Some of the more famous winners include Roger Staubach, Tony Dorsett, O.J. Simpson, Earl Campbell, and the only two-time winner, Archie Griffin.

The most significant innovation of the 1940's was the instigation of the "two platoon" system. Until then, it was normal for players to play the entire sixty minutes of a game, regardless of whether it was offensive or defensive actions. Coach Fritz Crisler of Michigan first started using offensive and defensive teams in 1945 to compensate for the inexperience of his players after the war. The idea caught on with other schools until the NCAA temporarily banned the practice in the 1950's by permitting only two substitutions after each play.

Today, though, specialists are an accepted part of the game. Players in college and professional ball concentrate either on defense or offense. Many teams also have special groups that participate only on kickoffs, punts and field goal attempts.

The NFL as we know it today began operating in the 1930's. The first NFL championship game was played in 1933 when the Chicago Bears defeated the New York

Giants 23-21. The championship game has been played every year since and is now known as the Super Bowl.

Pro football entered the modern era of incredible popularity with the 1958 NFL championship game. For the first time ever, two teams tied at the end of four 15-minute quarters and went into sudden-death overtime. The Baltimore Colts behind Johnny Unitas and Alan Ameche scored at 8:15 of overtime to defeat the New York Giants 23-17. Many fans still consider that the greatest football game ever played.

In 1960, hoping to break into the pro football market, the American Football League was formed. For six years, the two major leagues battled for top players and television exposure. A merger was concluded in 1966 and in 1967 the first Super Bowl game was played in Los Angeles, where Green Bay defeated Kansas City 35-10.

The great coach Vince Lombardi led his Packers to a second Super Bowl triumph in 1968 with a 33-14 romp over Kansas City. But in 1969 the old AFL proved they belonged in the NFL when the New York Jets, led by quarterback Joe Namath, shocked the heavily favored Baltimore Colts by a 16-7 score. The Super Bowl grew to be the number one single sports event in the United States. Today, the game attracts more than 100 million viewers on television. During the season, millions more watch the 28 NFL teams in person and on television.

The college game is just as popular; more than 30 million fans attend games each year. Millions more view games on the high school fields. The first secondary school game was played in 1875 and now more than 14,000 high schools and 700,000 teenage players compete.

The future of football continues to look bright. More than two million people play the game in youth programs, junior and senior high schools, colleges, universities and pros. Millions more watch games in person and on television. New rules and inventions are being developed to make the game safer and more enjoyable, thus helping to insure that football remains the number one sport in the United States today.

16

RULES

Some people have likened this game to chess, others to war. A game of skill, strength, size, speed and strategy, without doubt football is the most complex physical-contact sport played today. Entire books have been written about one particular offense or defense. But before a football player can begin studying the game, a basic under-standing of the rules is necessary.

Each level of football has differences in rules, but the basics are the same. For example, the playing field is a surface 360 feet (120 yards) long and 160 feet (53⅓ yards) wide. Goal lines are 10 yards from each end of the field, and these two 10-yard-wide areas are called endzones. The remaining 100 yards are lined across the width of the field every five yards. (See diagram for reference.)

At the back of the endzones, centered halfway between each sideline, are goal posts. The cross bar of the posts is 10 feet off the ground with uprights extending above the cross bar. Points are scored by kicking a ball between these uprights. In college, the distance between the uprights is 23 feet, 4 inches, while in the NFL, this width is 18 feet, 6 inches.

In both college and pro ball, small broken lines, called hash marks or inbound lines, divide the field into five yard segments. These lines are one yard apart and run the length of the field. In college ball, they are 53 feet, 4 inches from the sidelines, while the pros place their hash marks 70 feet, 9 inches from the sidelines. If a player goes out of bounds with the ball, or is stopped anywhere between the sideline and the hash marks, the next play always begins on the hash mark nearest the point where the play ended. This allows teams enough room to run their plays in any direction. Three yards from each goal line, in the center of the

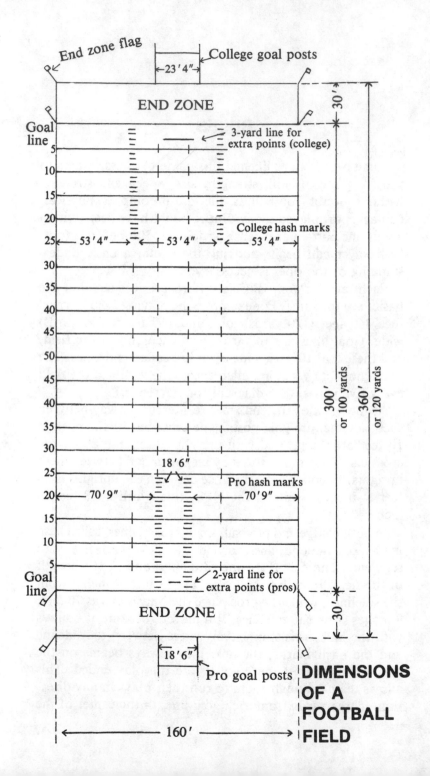

End zone flag

College goal posts

←23'4"→

END ZONE

30'

Goal line

5

3-yard line for extra points (college)

10

15

20

College hash marks

25 ←53'4"→ ←53'4"→ ←53'4"→

30

35

40

45

50

45

40

300' or 100 yards

360' or 120 yards

35

30

25

18'6"

20 ←70'9"→ ←70'9"→

Pro hash marks

15

10

5

Goal line

2-yard line for extra points (pros)

END ZONE

30'

18'6"

Pro goal posts

160'

DIMENSIONS OF A FOOTBALL FIELD

field (two yards for the pros), is a line from which all extra points are attempted after a touchdown.

The football is also standard for most levels of the game. Often called a pigskin, the ball actually contains nothing from a pig. Most balls are either made out of leather or rubber. A regulation football must be 11 to 11½ inches long, 28 to 28½ inches around from end to end, and between 21¼ and 21½ inches around the middle, although smaller balls are sometimes used for youngsters in junior programs. An official ball must be inflated with 12½ to 13½ pounds of air and weigh between 14 and 15 ounces. The color of the balls must be tan or brown and white lines may be added at either end of the ball to aid in visibility for night games.

Because football is a contact sport, proper protection is absolutely necessary. Most football programs require the following pieces of equipment to be worn by each player: helmet with face guard, mouth protector and chin strap, shoulder pads, hip pads, pants with thigh pads and knee pads, jersey, supporter, stockings and shoes. Many players also use rib pads, arm and elbow pads, neck pads and lots of tape for vulnerable joints such as the ankles.

There is a rhyme and reason for the jersey numbers of players. Most levels of football have a numbering system something like this: quarterbacks and kickers, 1-19; running backs and defensive backs, 20-49; centers and linebackers, 50-59; offensive guards and tackles and defensive linemen, 60-79; and ends, 80-89. At any one time on the playing field, there may be 11 players from each team. Occasionally smaller programs feature eight-man or six-man football, but we will concentrate exclusively on the game as played by 11 players.

The primary objective of the game is to score touchdowns, having a player carry or catch the ball across his opponent's goal line without being knocked down. Touchdowns are worth six points, with the opportunity to score one or two additional points. The ball is placed on the three-yard marker (two yards in pros) after a touchdown and the team has two options of scoring from this position.

Kicking the ball through the uprights of the goal posts is called an extra point or conversion, but a team may attempt to run the ball over the goal line for two points. (In the NFL, only one point may be scored on a conversion.)

Points may also be scored by kicking field goals. A field goal must be kicked from placement, that is with a player holding the ball on the field while the kicker attempts to boot it between the uprights of the goal posts. A successful field goal is worth three points.

The third manner of scoring is called the safety. A safety, worth two points, is scored by the team on defense when they tackle an opponent in their endzone.

The football game begins with a kickoff. Before the game, a referee will meet the team captains at the center of the field and toss a coin. The visiting team captain calls heads or tails. The team that wins the toss has the option of either kicking off, receiving the kick, or choosing which goal they wish to defend. Most teams choose to receive the kick when they win the toss, allowing them the first opportunity to score.

For simplification, let's say Team A wins the coin toss and elects to receive the kick. Then Team B will kickoff, and they choose which goal they wish to defend for the first quarter. Between that goal line and the 50 yard line is Team B's side of the field, with the other half Team A's territory.

To kick off, Team B lines up behind their own 40 yard line (35 in the pros) while Team A may line up anywhere behind the 50. Usually A will have five players up at the fifty, and the remainder scattered at various points back to where the return man (usually around the five yard line) expects the kick to come down.

The game starts when the kicker for B kicks the ball to Team A. Usually he will attempt to kick it as far as he can. When the receiver catches the ball, he attempts to run with it as far as possible toward A's goal line. If the kick goes into the endzone, the receiver may elect to run the ball out or he may "down" it for a touchback. A touchback isn't worth any points, but the ball is whistled dead and brought out to the 20 yard line where A begins play. If A's receiver elects to run the ball, the play is over as soon as he is brought down to the ground by the opposition (tackled).

Aside from kickoffs, every play begins at a line of scrimmage, determined by the spot where the previous play ended.On the offensive team, each player must line up behind the ball. The defense then lines up opposite the offensive team. The distance between the two teams, called the neutral zone, must be at least the length of the football.

Before each play, each team usually has a huddle to agree on the play they will run. When the teams line up at the line of scrimmage, the offensive team must have at least seven players on the line. No such requirement restricts the defensive team.

Every play from scrimmage begins with the center. Assume Team A has the ball. Lined up on either side of A's center are two guards (see diagram). The players immediately outside the guards are called tackles and the players directly outside the tackles are called ends. Many teams keep one of the ends right next to the tackle—he's called the tight end—and move the other end away from the line as a wide receiver or split end.

On most offensive plays, the center will hand the ball back to the quarterback who is directly behind him. This is called the snap. The position of the other three backs varies greatly according to the team's offense. Some teams like to keep all three backs directly behind the quarterback. (The wishbone and T formations are common examples.) Another option is to keep two backs behind the quarterback and split the other back between the tackles and wide receiver. This back is frequently called the flanker. There isn't space here to go into the many other possibilities of offensive formations.

At the start of an offensive series, Team A has four chances (called downs) to move the ball forward at least 10 yards toward B's goal line. If A makes 10 or more yards, it is called a first down and they have four more chances to move another 10 yards.

Each player begins with the center snapping the ball to

the quarterback who then has several options. He can choose to run with the ball himself, or he may hand the ball off to one of his backs. He may attempt a pass, by throwing the ball to one of his ends or one of his backs, but his teammate must catch the ball before it hits the ground or the play is over and the next down is played at the same line of scrimmage. There are also combinations of hand-offs and the pass, designed to fool the defense. If the play is a run, or if the quarterback completes his pass, the play is over at the point where the defense tackles the player with the ball. A play is also over if the player carries the ball out of bounds past the sidelines, and the new line of scrimmage is the point where he left the playing field.

In order to keep track of how far a team needs to move for a first down, three people on the sidelines handle what is called the chain. The chain is exactly 10 yards long with a tall stake at either end, held up by two of the chain crew. The third member holds the "box" which is a stake that marks the position of the ball at the start of each play and keeps track of the downs. If there is doubt about whether a team has earned a first down, officials use this chain for a measurement.

While the quarterback and backs attempt to advance the ball for Team A, the offensive linemen (center, guards, tackles and often the ends) try to block the defenders. A legal block is made by hitting an opponent with the shoulder and arms (but not the hands) and attempting to move him away from the ball carrier to keep him from making the tackle. Except on the line of scrimmage, blockers may only hit the front of a defender. Hitting a player from behind is called clipping and will cost the team a 15-yard penalty.

As Team B is defending A, there are two ways they can gain the ball for their offense besides holding A to less than 10 yards in four downs. One is through recovery of a fumble, which is when an offensive player drops the ball or has it knocked from his hands. Another way is by intercepting a pass, that is catching the ball that was thrown by a player on A.

If A doesn't lose the ball via fumble or interception and is unable to gain 10 yards in their first three attempts, they have the option of punting or attempting to gain the final yards. Unless A is deep in B territory, or they are behind late in the game, they will usually choose to punt. If they are close to B's goal and have a good kicker, they may choose instead to attempt a field goal.

For a punt, the kicker will stand 12 to 15 yards behind his center. The center snaps the ball to him and the kicker then attempts to kick it down field as deep as possible. The B team will have a man back ready to return the kick, and as on a kickoff, he will attempt to run the ball back as far as possible before being tackled or forced out of bounds. At that point, Team B will begin their series with four chances to gain at least 10 yards.

On defense, many variations may be used to try and confuse the offense. The standard pro defense, called the four-three, uses four defensive linemen, three linebackers and four defensive backs. (See diagram.) In recent years, a variation has been used called the three-four which uses three defensive linemen and four linebackers. Many high schools and colleges prefer other defenses, such as the five-two or six-one. In goal line defense or short yardage situations, it's common for a defense to put even more players on the line to try and prevent the offense from making those last one or two yards.

A football game is divided into four quarters of equal lengths (15 minutes in pro and college, 12 in high school, and less for younger levels of play). Teams will exchange ends of the field between the first two and last two quarters, with no change in the line of scrimmage or down. Between the two halves, usually a break of 20 minutes allows the teams to go into the locker rooms to rest and review strategy. The second half begins with a kickoff and the team that lost the coin toss at the start of the game has the first option to kick, receive or choose which goal they wish to defend.

Of course, the team with the most points at the end of the game is the winner. In case of a tie, the rules vary. The

OFFENSIVE AND DEFENSIVE POSITIONS

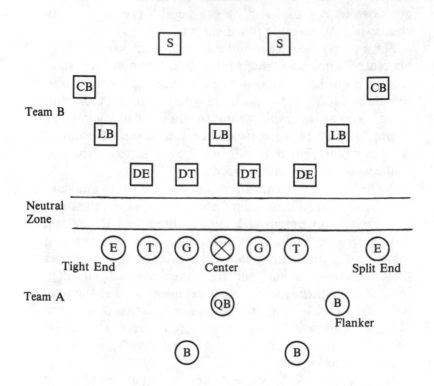

DEFENSE

Team B

Neutral Zone

Team A

Tight End   Center   Split End

Flanker

OFFENSE

Defense		**Offense**	
S	Safety	G	Guard
CB	Corner Back	T	Tackle
LB	Linebacker	E	End
DE	Defensive End	QB	Quarter Back
DT	Defensive Tackle	B	Back

NFL plays a 15-minute sudden-death overtime, and in playoffs, will continue with another 15-minute period if the game is still tied. Ties in college ball are kept as such. Rules vary in high school according to the state—some choosing to stay with the ties, others breaking the tie by giving each team a chance to score from the opponents 10-yard line.

Time is kept on a stopwatch or scoreboard clock. The clock is stopped whenever a player goes out of bounds with the ball, on incomplete passes, on penalties, or whenever the referee stops the clock. Each team usually is allowed three timeouts each half.

Depending on the level of play, anywhere from four to seven men are responsible for controlling a football game. These men are called officials with the referee in charge of the rest of the officiating crew. Other members of the crew are called by such titles as head linesman, line judge, back judge, field judge and umpire. Officials are responsible for marking the ball, keeping track of the clock, the downs, timeouts, and enforcing the rules.

When an official spots an infraction, he throws a yellow handkerchief, called a flag, and he informs the captain of the team against which the penalty was committed when the play is completed. Usually a team can choose whether or not to accept the penalty.

The following are some of the more common penalties:

1. Offside—when a player jumps across the line of scrimmage before the snap. Penalty: five yards and replay of down.
2. Illegal motion—usually a back moving toward the line of scrimmage before the snap. Penalty: five yards, replay of down.
3. Delay of game—offensive team takes more than 25 seconds to begin a play. Penalty: five yards.
4. Illegal forward pass—pass thrown beyond the line of scrimmage. Penalty: five yards or loss of down.
5. Intentional grounding—quarterback throws ball to an area without any players to avoid a big loss

(usually determined by proximity of potential receiver). Penalty: five yards, loss of down.

6. Offensive pass interference—receiver interferes with defender after ball leaves quarterback but before it arrives at defender. Penalty: fifteen yards and loss of down.

7. Defensive pass interference—defender interferes with receiver before ball arrives. Penalty: offense ball at spot of infraction. (In high schools, 15 yards and automatic first down.)

8. Personal foul—clipping, piling on, tackling out of bounds after ball is dead, grabbing face mask, roughing the kicker or passer, or any unnecessary roughness. Penalty: fifteen yards.

9. Unsportsmanlike conduct—abusive or insulting language or gestures. Penalty: fifteen yards.

10. Illegal use of the hands—such as holding. Penalty: fifteen yards.

When a penalty is called near the goal line such that the markoff of distance would exceed half the distance to the goal, the penalty is half the distance to the goal line. For example, if A is on offense on B's six yard line and B is offside, the penalty would be three yards—half the distance to the goal—rather than five yards.

There are many other penalties and rules we could mention, but understanding these basics will help you enjoy the game more. If you are playing football yourself, it is imperative that you take the time to learn the rules for the level of ball you play. Each organization has slightly different rules or interpretations, so take the time to learn them. This will help maximize your enjoyment of the game.

Glossary

(Note: This glossary is provided for the readers to clarify some of the terms used frequently in this book. It is by no means an exhaustive list.)

BASIC HITTING POSITION: Knees and hips flexed, head up and looking straight at opponent and arms cocked. Used for pass protection blocking and tackling.

COMEBACK: Pass pattern where receiver runs toward defender, then cuts back toward the sideline at a 45° angle toward the line of scrimmage.

CROSS BLOCK: Basic drive block in which lineman switches assignment with blocker next to him.

CURL: See "Hook".

DOWNFIELD: Toward the goal line.

DRIVE BLOCK: Basic block for offensive lineman on a running play where blocker hits a defender in the chest with his shoulder and moves him out of his area in order to make room for a runner. Also called a basic shoulder block.

FLAT: Area three to five yards across the line of scrimmage and toward the side-lines.

HOOK: Pass route in which receiver runs toward defensive man, then stops and turns back toward the quarterback for a pass.

INSIDE: Toward the center of the field.

JAB STEP: A short step in one direction, with the intention of going another direction.

KEY: Signs and tips that the defense looks for to determine what play the offense is running.

LANE: A five-yard wide area of responsibility that a football player has when defending on kickoffs and punt returns.

LINE OF SCRIMMAGE: Imaginary line between the offensive and defensive lines, determined by the placement of the football, where each play starts.

OPTION: Play initiated by the quarterback who has a choice of either handing off, running with the ball himself, or pitching to his halfback.

OUT: Pass pattern where receiver drives downfield, then cuts at a 90° angle toward the sideline.

OUTSIDE: Toward the sideline.

PENETRATION: When the defense forces itself into the offensive backfield.

PLAY ACTION: Play in which the quarterback fakes a handoff to a running back and drops back to pass.

POCKET: Protective cup around the quarterback on a pass play, formed by the offensive line.

POST PATTERN: Pass pattern in which receiver runs up the field, then cuts toward the center of the field, heading toward the goal posts.

PULL: Move in which offensive lineman makes a 90° pivot in the direction he's going and leaves his position in the line in order to lead a running play around end.

SCREEN: Play in which a short pass is thrown to receiver or running back behind a wall of offensive linemen who have pulled to lead the play.

SPRINTOUT: Play in which the quarterback can either run or pass, depending on the reaction of the defense.

STRIKING DISTANCE: About 18 inches between two opposing players.

STUTTER STEP: A flurry of steps to confuse a defender.

SWIM: Technique used by defensive linemen who pull down on the shoulder of an offensive lineman with one hand and use their free hand to pull their way past their opponent into the backfield.

SWING PASS: A pass play where the back runs within five yards of the sideline and then cuts upfield.

UP: Pass pattern where receiver runs straight upfield.

UPFIELD: Same as downfield--toward the goal line.

Running
Archie Griffin
Cincinnati Bengals

The Heisman Trophy is the ultimate individual award in college football—symbolizing the best football player in in the country. Until Archie Griffin won the award in 1974 and 1975, no one had ever won it twice.

When he graduated from Ohio State University, Archie had set an NCAA record for most yards rushing with 5,177 and most consecutive games gaining 100 or more yards—31. Those accomplishments made him a first round draft choice of the Cincinnati Bengals, despite question marks about his size—5' 9" and 189 pounds.

Griffin quickly dispelled those doubts by winning a starting job with the Bengals. In his rookie season, he gained 625 yards on 138 carries, including a 77-yard touchdown run against Kansas City. That run was the longest of the 1976 AFC season. In 1977 he carried 137 times for 549 yards and caught 28 passes for 240 additional yards.

Becoming a two-time Heisman Trophy winner didn't just happen. True, I am blessed with some great natural ability, but it took a lot of work to develop that ability in a way that would allow me to fulfill my potential. It also took a great team around me, including a great offensive line, to help me gain those yards and set those records.

When I was in junior high school, the counselor of our student council sat down with me and gave me three words to remember. I've never forgotten them. He told me that nothing would be accomplished in my football career, or in any other part of my life unless I had desire, dedication and determination.

Let me amplify those briefly. Desire means you want to accomplish something, and you want it enough to be willing to make whatever sacrifice is necessary to reach that goal. That's where your dedication comes in. That's the discipline to follow your training schedule, to master your techniques, to practice, to learn and listen to your coach. Add to that determination, which means you will never quit in doing whatever is necessary to reach your goal. These three D's—desire, dedication and determination are what made me a successful football player.

Everyone is born with a certain amount of innate abilities. But that doesn't mean you'll automatically use them. You need to work to develop those abilities. I happen to be blessed with speed and quickness. I think both are important if you want to be a running back, though you don't always need great speed to play the running back position.

It's hard for me to explain how I execute some of the moves I make on the football field. No one really taught them to me. I simply worked hard to develop my skills and experimented to find out what worked and what didn't. But let me give you a few of the techniques that have worked for me. They will help anyone who has to run with a football.

The first thing a running back needs to do is have a good stance. There are four types of stances: the two point, the three point square, the three point staggered, and the four point. I will explain the first three. The four point is rarely used except in something like a wishbone formation where the fullback is lined up right behind the quarterback. A four point only allows you to move straight ahead. The other three stances allow you to move equally well in any direction—forward, laterally to either side or backward.

In the two point stance, your feet are perpendicular to the line of scrimmage and even toe to toe, about shoulder width. Your hands rest on the knees with the knees slightly bent. Your head is facing straight ahead. You've probably observed O.J. Simpson using this stance. The advantage of this is you can see the defense clearly.

In the three point square stance, the feet are again perpendicular to the line of scrimmage and even with your shoulders. The weight is equally distributed on both feet. You bend over until your four fingers (either right or

Two point stance

Three point staggered stance

Three point square stance

left hand, whichever is most comfortable) are touching the ground with your knees slightly bent. But don't put any weight on the fingers. This is a good balanced stance and effective for just about anything the quarterback calls.

For the three point staggered stance, the toe of one foot is lined up opposite the middle of your other foot. Again the feet are shoulder width. If your right foot is back, then you lean over and place your right fingers on the ground; it's just the opposite if your left foot is back. There will be a little weight on the finger tips this time, but keep it to a minimum.

Whichever stance you use, you should use it consistently. Don't shift your weight or stance according to the play or else the defense will be able to read you and anticipate the play you'll be running.

When you come out of your stance to take a handoff, there are two ways you can accept the ball from the quarterback. One is the breadbasket, the other is by forming a pocket. I prefer the pocket method because it gives the quarterback a better target, and in my opinion, there is less chance of a fumble.

But let me describe both ways. For the breadbasket handoff, put the knife edge of your hands together—that is your two little fingers line up. Your hands are cupped in close to your stomach, with your arms resting across the front of your stomach. The quarterback hands you the ball nose first, and as he places it in your hands, they will naturally close around it.

Breadbasket

Pocket handoff

For the pocket handoff, I'll describe it going to the quarterback's right. Your left elbow is up just below chest level, and your arm extends across your chest with the hand facing down. Your fingertips should touch your right bicep. Your right elbow is down at waist level and your palm faces up as your right arm is extended across your belt.

Putting the ball away

After the ball is placed in the pocket, the right hand covers the point of the ball and the left hand moves the other point deep into the crook of your right elbow. This method is just the opposite if you're going to the quarterback's left. With both forms of handoff, you should automatically put the ball away before you do anything else.

Whichever side of the field you're running on, the football should be in the arm on that side. In other words, if you are running toward the right, the ball is in your right arm. The reason is that most of the tacklers come at you from the opposite direction and therefore you can protect the ball from them.

If you switch direction, you can switch the arm you're holding the ball by returning to your pocket. Say the ball is in your right arm. To switch, bring your left hand across the top of the football and grab the nose of the ball in the crook of your elbow. Then use your right hand to guide the ball into your left elbow. It's a smooth switch and there's little chance of fumble once you've mastered it. However, you should never change hands with the football if you are in a crowd.

Always carry the football tucked away in the manner I've described. Never hold it like a loaf of bread as some backs do—with the ball in the palm of the hand and out away from the body. That is a cardinal sin. If the ball is out in front of you, anyone can come along and knock it loose. You can even lose the ball if you're not hit because you don't have control of it. So every time you have the ball, tuck it away.

When you take a handoff, you should be looking for your hole. It's the quarterback's job to put the ball in your hands. You need to give him the target. You should practice accepting a handoff enough so you don't have to look at the ball. Instead, let the quarterback give you the ball and you look for the hole.

Usually when you're running, you will follow a blocker. It is important to make sure you're a proper distance from your blocker, and the best way to do that is to put your hand lightly on his back. With your arm stretched out behind the blocker, you are at the perfect distance. Then whichever way the blocker goes, you cut behind him.

One thing that helps me know how to follow my blocker is to watch his head. If his head is on the left side of the person he's blocking, then I run to his left. If I were to go on his right, it would be easy for the tackler to slip his block and get me.

It is important to hit your hole moving straight ahead, never at an angle. This way you meet force with force. If you're moving at an angle, it's easier for a tackler to knock you backward. You simply don't have the momentum. When you move straight upfield, you have a better chance of making some yards. You can then make a move on the linebacker. Or if you're hit, you can move forward on the tackle.

Breaking a tackle using spin out technique

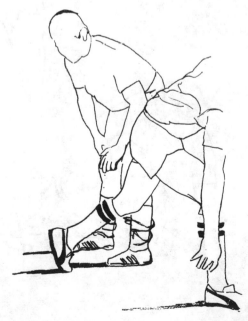

It's hard for me to explain how to break a tackle. I do it without thinking. The key is to run hard and never stop moving your legs. There are two things you can work on that are basic for breaking a tackle. One is called the spin out, and I'll call the other the hand spring.

First the spin out. This is a good technique to use when you're in a one-on-one situation. First you want to be head on to the tackler. When you're within one yard of him, you choose a side. If you choose to go to his left, you drop your right shoulder and make contact. The tackler wants to get his arms around you and you don't want him to. So as you make contact, you spin around to your left and keep moving.

Breaking a tackle using hand spring technique

The hand spring is good to use when you're in a crowd. The key here is to keep low and move straight downfield toward the primary tackler. Again, you pick a side and dip your shoulder. You would like to miss him entirely if possible, but you'll usually make some contact. But since you're moving forward, you'll be falling forward. As you fall, use your free hand to hit the ground and spring off of it and continue moving.

An easy way to practice the hand spring is to bend over and put your weight on one hand and run in a circle around that hand.

Cutting is a major part of running. If you want to make yardage and also survive in football without too many straight ahead collisions, you need to be quick with your feet. There's a little drill that I do to work on my cuts. I run on a football field and every time I come to a line, I cut 90° and run up that line about five yards, then cut back another 90° up field until I come to the next line five yards further and I cut again, etc. It's a good conditioning drill and it will help you on your cuts.

I also recommend lots of exercise to help with your footwork, especially running through tires and jumping rope.   One final thing to keep in mind. Sometimes instead of a handoff, you take a pitchout. In my first game at Ohio State, I was so anxious to find my hole that I fumbled a pitchout from our quarterback. The ball had actually hit my hands, but I forgot to keep my eye on it. When you're taking a pitchout, keep your eye on the ball until you've put it away. Catch the ball the same way you would a pass. (See Charlie Sanders' Chapter on catching the football.)

I'll never forget that first game I played for Ohio State. It was the first year freshmen were eligible. The night before, I prayed for a chance to play. I got my chance at the end of the first quarter, when we were down 7-0. I played two and a half quarters, gained 239 yards and left the game to a standing ovation. When I got to the sidelines, I got on my knees and thanked God for the opportunity He had given me.

I believe what the Bible says is true: "Delight yourself in the Lord; and He will give you the desires of your heart" (Psalm 37:4). There is a lot of pressure playing the level of football I've played. But I've found that the Lord can ease my mind and relieve me of the pressure.

No matter what a person ends up doing in life, whether he plays football, is a doctor, or whatever, he should first delight in the Lord. He should put God first. Then he should apply desire, dedication and determination toward becoming the best that he can be in his chosen field.

Passing
Craig Morton
Denver Broncos

After thirteen professional seasons, Craig Morton finally enjoyed a season in the sun. In 1977, he led the Denver Broncos into the playoffs for their first time with a 12-2 record. Then he helped engineer wins over Pittsburgh and Oakland to land the Mile High City in the Super Bowl. There, against his old teammates, the Dallas Cowboys, the Denver dream ended with a 27-10 loss.

But that disappointment did nothing to diminish Morton's achievements. He completed 51.6% of his passes in 1977 for 1,929 yards and 14 touchdowns. And he led the AFC with fewest interceptions, only eight. In 1978, Morton's completion of 54.7% of his 267 passes for 1,802 yards and 11 touchdowns was key in the Broncos second win of their AFC Western Division.

Morton was a first round draft choice out of California by the Dallas Cowboys in 1965. He played nine full seasons with the Cowboys before being traded to the New York Giants mid-way through the 1974 season. He was traded again to the Broncos prior to the '77 season. During his career, Morton has played in 166 games, and thrown 2,713 passes, completing 1,423 for a completion percentage of 52.4%. His completions have covered 19,744 yards and included 134 touchdowns.

Most people think that to be a good passer you need a strong arm. That's not necessarily true. I've known quarterbacks who could throw harder and farther than I can, but they've never played professional football. There's a lot more to passing than just being able to throw hard.

Some situations call for the soft touch. You certainly don't want to fire the ball on a short pass to a halfback in the flat. You need to be able to throw a variety of distances, using different touches and positions to cover any situation.

Everyone has a little different way of throwing. I don't do it the same as everyone else. The way you throw needs to be comfortable for you and fit your physical capabilities.

For example, on the grip of the football, the standard instruction is to have the last two fingers of your passing hand over the laces. But if your hands are small, that's difficult to do, especially with a regulation NFL football. So rather than dictate that you hold it the conventional way, I think you should hold the ball in whatever way is comfortable for you.

But there are a couple of principles in determining your grip. You need to hold it with your fingers, not in the palm of your hand. That means you will probably hold it on the back one third of the ball. When I grip the ball, my index finger is almost on the nose of the football.

Before we get any further into passing, there is one basic point I need to make. On every snap from center, the quarterback must pull the ball into his stomach as if he was handing off, even if he intends to pass the ball. Every play must start from this position.

When you pass, as you start back into the pocket, you bring the football up from your stomach to chest level. Keep holding the ball with both hands, and don't take your non-throwing hand off until the last possible moment. That way you minimize the chance of dropping the ball or having it knocked from your hands.

As far as your footwork, you need to remember that you will only have three seconds to get your pass off.

Therefore, the quickest way to get back is to run back while keeping your eyes on the defense. This way, you're really running sideways. To do this, step back from the center with your right foot (if you're right-handed) and then follow with your left. The idea is that you are running back while your head is still facing downfield.

If you're throwing a quick pass, you take one step with your left foot, another with your right, plant and throw. That's the three-step set up. There are also five-step and seven-step set ups according to the situation. On all of them, your last step will always be with your right foot. When you complete that step, you plant that right foot and hop forward. The reason for this is to get you in an upright position and help you keep your balance. It also helps your offensive line as you are now moving up into the pocket. Your tackles will have an easier time keeping those defensive ends off of you.

When you throw, the exact arm motion will again depend on what's comfortable for you. Some passers like to throw straight overhand. Others prefer a three-quarters position and follow through. I don't suggest you throw under three-quarters. A sidearm throw stands a good chance of being knocked down by a defensive lineman. Always throw three-quarters or higher.

The key to good strong throws is in the legs, not in the arms. If you throw only with your arm, you'll put tremendous strain on it after a while, and you won't have as much power. Your legs and hips actually control the velocity of the pass. You need to push off with your back foot and follow through much as a baseball pitcher does, though not quite as exaggerated.

As you throw, you aim with your lead foot toward your target. When you release the football, your fingers actually leave the ball one at a time. If all your fingers left the ball at the same time, the effect would be a knuckle ball with no spin. To get a good spiral, your little finger comes off the ball first, followed by your ring and middle fingers, then your thumb and lastly your index finger.

But don't worry too much about that. If you're releasing

the ball properly, your fingers should wind up pointing straight at your intended target and your thumb pointing toward the ground.

These are the basics. From here there isn't a whole lot I can say except you need to practice many, many hours. Repetition is the only way you can learn to pass. You need to learn what your strengths and limitations are. You need to know how far you can throw the ball and how to throw it in different situations.

The best way to perfect your passing game is to work with your receivers. When you throw, you should usually aim for a receiver's chest. That way if you're a little off target, he has some room to adjust. But you should also practice throwing to different spots so you become accurate. For example, sometimes you want to throw the ball at a receiver's knees in order to minimize the risk of an interception.

Throwing a ball through a tire is one way to improve your accuracy. But also you can have a receiver call out a spot for you to aim at, say to his right shoulder or his left knee. I do this quite often.

Also, I suggest you get used to throwing the ball in all kinds of different situations and positions. The more unusual body positions you can throw from, the better prepared you are for a game, because the defense will not always let you stand in the pocket and get off a picture perfect pass. Sometimes you'll have to scramble and throw on the run. Occasionally you may even throw a pass when you're being tackled.

One of the most difficult aspects of passing is throwing on the run. There is one key here that will help you in this situation—keep your shoulders parallel to the line of scrimmage. If you are facing straight downfield, you will have much more control on your pass. This is especially important if you're moving to your left (for a right-hander). You don't want to be throwing across your body. Get your shoulders facing straight downfield.

One thing many quarterbacks have a problem with is handling pressure. It is difficult to throw a pass when some big defensive linemen are barreling down on you. But you can't worry about them because you already have plenty to think about. You should be concentrating on your receivers and the coverage of the defensive backs and linebackers. It's the job of your offensive line to take care of the defensive rush.

Timing is crucial to successful passing. That's why I start working with my receivers in May, three months before we go to training camp. This is so important because on most pass patterns you will throw the ball the instant the receiver makes his cut, sometimes even before he makes his cut. So he won't be looking at you. When he turns, the ball will be on its way. Therefore receiver and quarterback must be thinking together and knowing what the other is going to do.

The deep pass, the bomb, is the most spectacular play in football. Even if it is incomplete, it usually brings a reaction from the crowd and shakes up a defense. The best way to throw a long pass is to lead your receiver. Put the ball up in the air and let your man run under the ball. Again, this requires a lot of practice. You need to know the speed of your receiver, and your own limitations as to how far you can throw the ball. Don't try to throw a 50-yard pass if you can only throw it 40 yards.

Many young players like to know what they can do to strengthen their arms. I don't recommend that you use weights for your arm. I relied on my natural body growth and simply throwing the football. When I got tired, I stopped throwing that day and rested my arm. I think that's the best way to do it.

I've been throwing a football since I was in fourth grade. The only position I've ever played is quarterback. If you want to be a quarterback, throw the ball every chance you get. Success in passing is mainly repetition. You need to throw and throw. When I was in grade school, there was always someone to throw a ball to. You can throw to your friends, your neighbors, your dad, to anyone who will catch for you.

But don't think you have to throw the ball farther than

everyone else to be a quarterback. I think it's more important that your receivers have confidence in you. You don't throw deep all that often, so if you can execute the short and medium range passes effectively on a consistent basis, you'll be playing a lot of football.

I've always enjoyed playing football, and I hope to be able to play for a few more years. But in 1977, something happened that allowed me to enjoy it even more. I accepted Jesus Christ into my life. Since I've become a Christian, I have had more confidence and concentration than ever before. And beyond that, I've been able to accept whatever happens on the football field, whether it's winning the AFC championship, as we did against Oakland, or losing the Super Bowl, as we did against Dallas in 1978.

I think it is important to give praise to God no matter what happens. And I hope to do that from now on in my career.

Blocking
John Hannah
New England Patriots

It was no surprise to Coach "Bear" Bryant of Alabama when John Hannah won the Mack Bulldog Award for the first time in 1977 as the outstanding offensive lineman in the National Football League. The Bear believes that the 6'2", 265 pound guard is the best offensive lineman he has ever coached. During his senior season, Hannah captured every award available to an offensive lineman in the United States.

Hannah was the fourth player chosen in the 1973 draft and the first choice of the New England Patriots. He moved right into the starting lineup and proved he belonged among the best in the NFL. He made the "Pro Football Weekly" and "Football Digest" all-Rookie teams, was the team's rookie of the year and MVP on offense. The next season he was named to several all-AFC teams and, along with tackle Leon Gray, gave the Pats one of the best left sides in the league. In 1976, their blocking helped the team gain 2,948 yards rushing. In 1977 and '78, Hannah was elected to most every all-pro team.

Coach Paul "Bear" Bryant taught me a very important lesson during my sophomore year at Alabama. We were preparing to play Southern California in a big intersectional game. It was early in the season, and we were having a long practice in weather that was exceedingly hot and humid. It was so miserable that five players had to be taken to the hospital for heat stroke.

I was feeling sorry for myself under these conditions and wondering when practice would finally end. In the midst of my self-pity, Coach Bryant came up behind me, gave me a hard boot in the rear end and told me to get moving. The next day, he called a team meeting before practice and I'll never forget what he said: "Gentlemen, you've just learned that the human body is an amazing machine. You think you're going to die out there on the field, but you won't. Your body is so made up that you'll pass out first. You learned yesterday that you can do more than you think you can."

I've never forgotten that lesson, and it is really one of the keys to successful blocking. The other is proper technique. But once you learn the techniques, it really comes down to how much you're willing to work.

There are two basic blocks that you need to learn. One is the drive block; the other is the pass protection block. For each the stance is the same. So first, I will explain the basic stance. This is the most important thing for an offensive lineman to learn. If you don't have a proper stance, the rest of these techniques won't help you.

The purpose of a stance is to allow you mobility to move forward or laterally or backward. If you have too much weight forward, you'll most likely get beat on pass blocking. If your weight is too far back, you'll be unable to launch an effective drive block. So a good stance is *balanced*.

There are four elements to a good, balanced stance. First, your feet should be about shoulder width apart. Second, your back must be level, that is parallel to the ground. Third, you must keep your head up. And fourth, you should keep your rear end down, not stuck up in the air.

Balanced stance

You should practice being in this stance so it feels comfortable. In most cases, you should use a three point stance. With a four point stance, the only thing you can do is drive ahead. With a three point, your weight can be more evenly distributed so you can move any direction. When I get in my stance, I put a lot of weight on my right hand that's on the ground. I don't suggest you do that. You should put only enough weight on it so that you can still move forward or backward.

With this stance in mind, let me describe a proper drive block. First, you must focus your eyes on your target—your opponent's chest, right under his shoulder pads. On the snap, you take a short step with the foot that is closest to your opponent. For example, if your opponent is to your right, you will step with your right foot and make contact with him as you take your second step with the left foot. You do just the opposite if your opponent is on your left.

This first step is very important because it allows you to build up momentum that is essential for a good drive block. Your first step is very short, no more than three or four inches. On the second step, you hit your man.

The secret here is to beat your man off the ball. If you don't, he'll beat you. An offensive lineman has to be fast—for about three yards. He doesn't have to run a hundred yard dash fast, but on his first step, he should be as fast as any running back. There is no easy way to develop this except lots of hard work. You should practice hard getting the jump off the snap of the ball.

When you fire off after the snap, you must keep the same stance position until you make contact. Don't stand up and expect to drive block. You must keep your back level to the ground and your head up. The reason for this is that your power is in your legs, not your upper body. If you have good strong legs, and you stay in the proper position, you'll be able to beat your man.

Drive block

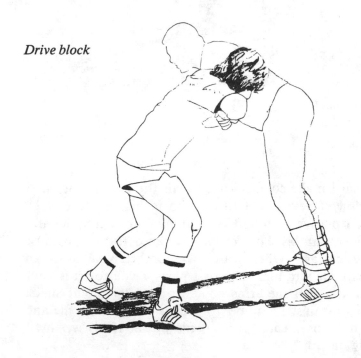

Drive block

When I make contact I try to hit the man in the chest or below. I never want to hit him in his shoulder pads. He can push me around if I hit him up there. But if I hit underneath his shoulder pads, I can defeat him because I have leverage. When you make contact, your hips and legs explode into him. The first part of you to hit is your forehead. Then the arms come up and your butt sinks. When I do this, I am able to get his weight onto me and limit his movement. He loses his power if his weight is resting on you.

The two men I have the most problems blocking in the NFL are Jerry Sherk (Cleveland) and Steve Furness (Pittsburgh), and it's because they play so low. It's hard to get under their shoulder pads. The key to beating your opponent is to hit his chest, underneath his shoulder pads.

Once you've made contact and exploded your hips and legs, it simply becomes a matter of who wants to win the battle the most. That means you keep following through with your technique. The key is to keep driving your legs for all you're worth. Stop moving your legs and your man will beat you. If you're in a stalemate, keep moving your legs and driving, because when your running back hits the hole, the defender will find it difficult to reach him since some of his weight is resting on you. If he reaches for the back, you should be able to move him.

That's all there is to a drive block. I know it doesn't sound terribly complicated—it isn't. Learn the basics and then it simply comes down to your desire. A lineman's objective here is to create a hole for the running back to go through. If your running back goes through the hole, you've done your job.

As far as pass blocking, you keep the same stance. Your stance should never change. The temptation on a pass block is for the lineman to put more weight on his legs. If you do this, the defense will pick it up and be able to tell what the play is.

The main problem with pass blocking is that defensive linemen can use their hands. That gives them an advantage. However, you only have to keep them out of the backfield for three seconds. That should be enough time for the quarterback to complete his pass.

On the snap, you immediately set up in a basic hitting position. To get into the basic hitting position, put your hands on your knees, with the knees slightly bent. Then the hands come to the proper cocked position which will depend on the level of football you're in. Keep your head up facing your opponent and your hips flexed ready to uncoil.

Basic hitting position

The key now is to stay low and keep the legs bent so you can move quickly in any direction. Your eyes should focus on your man's chest. He can fake with his head, his feet, his shoulders. But he can't fake his whole body. So I look at his numbers. Occasionally you get a defender who turns his whole body, but you can deal with that when the situation arises. That's one purpose of practice the week before a game, to study the tendencies of your opponent.

In most cases you let the defensive man make the first contact. You act a lot like a shock absorber. Your job is to stay low and *keep in front of him.* Give ground grudgingly. Your job is to stay between your man and the quarterback for three seconds. Again, it is simply a matter of who wants it the most. Does he want to get by you more than you want to stop him? If so, you'll get beat.

There are two other blocks I want to mention briefly. The drive block and pass block are used in the offensive line. These other two blocks are downfield blocks. One is a running block, the other is a cross body block.

In order to execute a good running block, you need a back who will stay right behind you. Your job is to run straight at the man you are to block, aiming right for the middle of his chest. Usually in this case, the man you're blocking is smaller than you, and therefore probably quicker and trickier. So you want to force him to go to one side of you or the other. He certainly won't want to meet you head on. When he chooses that side, you simply hit him and move him further in the direction he chose. The back should go past you on the other side. The key to the success of this block is a running back who will stay close to you, because all you are doing is getting in the way of the defensive back.

On the cross body block your charge toward the defender is exactly the same. You must not commit yourself until you are about eighteen inches away. You must be right on top of him, almost stepping on his toes. If you're on the right side of the field, you throw your head to the right and throw your left hip into him. The key is to make him think you're going to run over him. Be sure and bring your hip into the defender about belly button level.

These techniques are all very important, but keep in mind that, after you learn them, it comes down to who has the most desire. If I get beat most of the time in a game, then I have to ask two questions. First, did I have a problem with my technique? Second, did I have a problem in my heart? If it's not the first, then it's definitely the second.

If I begin to feel tired during a game and feel like letting up, I let the goal posts be a reminder to me. Every time I see the goal posts, they remind me of my Lord Jesus Christ and what He went through for me. He experienced excruciating torture and died a horrible death in order that I might have forgiveness of sin. If He did all that for me, then I certainly can give everything I have for Him on the football field.

There are a lot of ups and downs in a football game. There are high points and low points. But if you're going to achieve your full potential, then you need a stabilizing factor that won't be upset by the circumstances. For me, Christ is that stabilizing factor. The goal posts remind me that on every single play I must give my utmost, I must do my very best. I must work as hard as I can because of what He did for me.

Center
Rick Saul
Los Angeles Rams

It took six years for Rich Saul to become the starting center for the Los Angeles Rams, but only two more years to earn a reputation as one of the best centers in pro football. The 6'3" 250 pounder from Michigan State replaced fifteen year veteran Ken Iman in 1975, and in 1976, '77 and '78 he was named to play in the Pro Bowl game. Twice he was voted all-NFL Center by UPI.

With the Rams, Saul has been a starter on teams that have had 12-2, 10-3-1, 10-4 and 12-4 regular season records while winning the Western Division title each year. Prior to 1975, Saul proved valuable to the team by backing up at center, guard, tackle, tight end, and was even considered as a candidate for linebacker. He also contributed on the Ram's special teams. In his nine seasons of pro football, Saul has never missed a regular season game, appearing in 128 consecutive contests.

For anyone who's going to play center, there is one thing he must never forget. His number one priority on every play is the snap. Without a clean snap, the play has virtually no chance of succeeding. For that reason, I feel a center should be as familiar with the ball as the quarterback, running back or end.

A good center is similar in many respects to a middle linebacker. He doesn't need speed, but he must be quick, and he must be strong because he frequently has heavier men playing over him. And he needs to be intelligent. On most pro teams, the center is the one who calls the blocking assignments for the offensive line.

But back to the snap. That is your first priority on every play. If you snap for punts and place kicks as well as regular downs, you will handle the ball more than anyone else on the team, so you should feel comfortable holding a ball. You've probably seen pitchers walk around with a baseball in their hands, or a basketball player who carries a ball with him and dribbles it every chance he gets. These athletes are simply getting used to the feel of the ball they use. That's the way a center should be. He should throw, catch and handle a football every chance he gets.

As I explain the basic snap to the quarterback, the first thing to keep in mind is your stance. As you lean over the ball on a typical play, your stance is as square as the other offensive linemen, except because both of your hands are on the ball, your feet should be flat on the ground and slightly wider than shoulder width, so as to feel comfortable. You need to be balanced though so you can move in any direction.

You'll be tempted to lean too far forward in this position. But if you do, then the only thing you can do is move forward. If it takes a moment for you to set up after the snap because you're leaning too far forward, then your defensive man will play you like a rag doll. So it's important to keep your balance.

For the snap the laces should face straight up. Both of your hands go on the ball. Your thumbs should be on top of the laces, and your fingers on the side of the ball.

When you snap to the quarterback, your left hand comes up for protection, and the right takes the ball and makes a natural, counterclockwise, half turn. You simply bring the ball up to the quarterback and he catches the ball with his fingers on the laces. That's important. The laces should always hit his fingers so he doesn't have to worry about where they are when he sets up to pass.

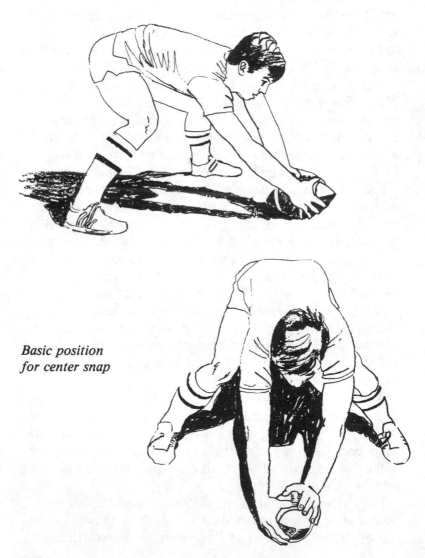

*Basic position
for center snap*

Snap for quarterback

That's all there is to the technique. The rest is simply practice. You have to work with your quarterback because each one has his own way of taking the ball. Some put their hands deep into your crotch; others like them back on your buttocks. It's your responsibility to put the ball where he wants it. It looks automatic in the game, but it requires hundreds of practice snaps to perfect it.

The most common mistake young centers make is they move before the snap. You must not move any part of your body until you move the ball. There are two reasons for this: one, you'll be called for illegal procedure, and two, you may get knocked into the backfield by the middle guard keying on your movement. Another mistake is that many kids move their buttocks too soon. You can't move it until the quarterback has the ball. It must be there for a proper exchange. You can move forward some because the quarterback will move forward a little with you. But otherwise, keep your stance the same.

Most bad snaps occur because either the quarterback or the center is overly anxious. Never take the snap for granted. The quarterback should keep his hands on your buttocks until he has the ball, and you should not move until the ball is in his hands.

Once the snap is made, then you can think about blocking. There are three situations you will face: 1) blocking the man directly over you on the line, 2) blocking a man over you but behind the line, and 3) blocking a man to either side of you.

The blocking techniques for a center are the same as John Hannah described. That means on a drive block, your initial step is never more than about two or three inches. If you take too long a step, you'll be off balance. If you take a short step, you can read the situation and make contact on the second step.

It is important to always lead your block with your head, and then let your hands follow. Never lead with the shoulder. If you do, you'll most likely miss your man because it will be easy for him to evade you. As for all offensive linemen, you must be under control. For example, suppose your job is to block the middle linebacker. If you charge out too fast, it will be easy for him to use your weight against you and simply throw you out of his way. So you need to explode out and yet keep control.

On pass blocking the technique is the same as for the guards and tackles. Here, let me simply say that if you stop moving your feet, you're dead. The same is true with a drive block. Keep making short choppy steps with your feet about shoulder width apart. The other thing to keep in mind is to stay low. I aim for the bottom of a guy's numbers. If he is low then you need to get down and bang helmets and root him out.

As a center you need to realize the importance of your position. Your blocks are very important because if you miss a block, your man can almost always make the tackle. An offensive tackle can miss his block and if the play is on the other side of the field, it may not make too much difference. That's not true with a center.

On field goals and punts, you've probably seen many a bad snap cost a team a good kick. The snap is a critical part of the kicking game. The technique is the same for both punts and field goals. The snap motion is exactly the same as throwing the football. That's why I recommend you get used to handling a football—to throwing it around a lot.

If you can throw a spiral pass, then you can execute a spiral snap. If your passes wobble, your snaps will too. The best way to get the feel of a proper snap is to stand up straight and cock your arm with the football at your head, just as if you were going to pass it. Then, in this position, bend at the waist and knees until the ball touches the ground. Now you're ready to snap. You simply throw the ball between your legs. It's exactly the same motion as a pass.

A good throw with a football is the opposite of throwing a curve in baseball. With a baseball, your wrist rolls out and your thumb ends up on top, pointing to the sky. With a football, your wrist moves inward and your thumb ends up pointing to the ground.

Position for snap on kicks

I suggest you use the other hand as a guide on the snap. Thus when you complete your snap, your hands should be between your legs, side by side. If they aren't even, then your snap will be off line. You might get the feel of this by passing the ball using your other hand as a guide.

You should look between your legs when you snap. Don't worry about the defense. Remember that your number one priority is to snap the ball. If you don't do that right, then your blocking won't matter anyway.

On your snap your hands wind up between your legs, so you won't be able to help much on blocking. As soon as the ball moves, the defense will be moving so you're simply going to have to absorb the blow on long snaps. On punts, I simply figure I have to go down field and cover and I don't worry about blocking except to help wherever I can. On field goals the shortest route to the kicker is over you, so you'll have to take the punishment.

Becoming a good center is hard work. You not only have to be a good blocker like the rest of the line, but you have to handle the ball well. There is no other secret besides lots of practice and hard work.

I believe there are three kinds of people, and you'll see them all in the lower levels of football. There are those people who watch things happen, those who make things happen, and those who wonder what happened. The first and third kind of person never last long in football.

My example on the football field is the person of Jesus Christ. As I read about Him in the Bible, I see that He made things happen. When people were using the temple for money-making purposes, Christ went in and threw them out. Everywhere He went people followed Him because they knew with Him things were going to happen.

I feel I can make things happen on the football field the way Christ did in His work. Following Christ has given me a basis for my life on and off the football field. I play to please Him. There is no way I will jeopardize that in order to please someone else. Serving Christ is the most exciting kind of life I can imagine.

Offensive Guard
George Buehler
Cleveland Browns

Though not as well-known as his counterpart on the left side, Gene Upshaw, George Buehler was a regular on the Oakland Raiders offensive line for more than seven years. Beginning the 1978 season, he had played in 112 consecutive regular season games. In 1974 he was honored as the Raiders' "Lineman of the Year." During the 1978 season, Buehler was traded to the Cleveland Browns.

With the Raiders, Buehler helped anchor an offensive line that was considered one of the best in professional football. In Super Bowl XI, they helped set a Super Bowl record of 266 yards rushing and 429 yards total offense. The strong and durable guard stands 6′ 2″ tall and weighs 270 pounds. He was the Raiders' second pick in the 1969 draft after graduating from Stanford University.

Most people casually watching a football game probably can't tell the difference between an offensive guard and tackle. They just know there are four big men inside whose jobs are to move the defense out of the way. But the intricacies of each position are important and, while the basic skills of the guard and tackle are the same, their assignments and the problems they have to face are often quite different.

For example, on pass protection the guard has less margin for error because the defensive tackle has a shorter route to the quarterback. The defensive end has to travel a longer path to the quarterback and the tackle can often ride him out of the play. That's not to say it is an easy job. It's a different technique.

On a running play an offensive tackle has to hold his blocks longer on runs to the outside, because it takes longer for the back to get outside. Because of this the guards generally do more pulling than the tackles. In this chapter I'd like to explain three common plays you'll have to make as a guard: 1) pulling, 2) the cross block, and 3) the trap.

First let me explain the difference. On the pull the guard leaves his position on the line of scrimmage and goes outside the tight end to block for a runner on a sweep. On a cross block the guard's assignment is to block either the defensive end or middle linebacker (facing a 4-3 defensive set)—in other words, the man normally blocked by either the tackle or center. On the trap you usually run to the opposite side of the line to block the defensive end or tackle.

For proper pulling technique you need a square stance. Some guards like to use a staggered stance, with the toe of one foot even with the heel of your other foot. Everything else is the same. If you feel more comfortable with this stance, you have to use it on every play. If you use it only for a pull, the defense will pick it up and read the play. Also, some players tip a play by looking in the direction they're going to pull. Always keep your eyes on the man in front of you.

Whatever stance you use needs to be balanced. You

shouldn't have too much weight forward on your hand. I can tell my stance is right if, when I lift my hand off the ground, I still can stay on my feet without falling forward. This way, I am free to move in any direction necessary.

In a drive block you take a very short first step. The same is true when you pull. If you are pulling right, you need to pivot your right foot about a 90° angle to open your stance. You can even move the foot back an inch or two.

At this point a lot of coaches say you should throw your right elbow back in order to twist your body into the direction you want to pull. I think that's slower for me than if I keep my upper body facing straight ahead and rotate my hips to the right. If I do this, the upper body will come naturally and I can move a little quicker. This is important because the longer you take to pull out, the more likely you are to be hit by the defensive tackle which can destroy the timing of the play.

First step for pulling guard

When you pivot, you want the weight of your body to be out over that pivot foot. Do not stand up. This is the most common mistake. You want to keep your back level to the ground. With your weight over your right foot, the natural thing in order to keep your balance is to move your left foot. If you were to freeze in this position, you would look like a sprinter coming out of the blocks.

Your run behind the line of scrimmage should be about one to two yards. It is important to run a little into the back field in order to have an easier turn when it's time to move upfield. If you move straight up the line of scrimmage, then you have to make a very severe cut and to do it you lose much of your momentum.

On the pull you want to go outside the tight end. From there it depends on who you're going to hit. Usually you will either go inside and block a linebacker, or you will go outside and block a defensive back.

If you are blocking the defensive back, then your running back will want to go inside and your job is to take the defender outside, towards the sideline. Again, assuming the play is being run right, you want to hit the man off your right foot and shield the ball carrier with your left step. To do this correctly it is crucial that you not stretch in order to make contact. You practically want to step on the defender's foot before you explode off your right foot. When you hit him you swing your left foot around so the ball carrier can go by.

If you have to go inside to block a linebacker, then your running back will want to run outside you, so your block is just the opposite. You explode off your left foot and protect with your right step.

Control is important to keep in mind when you are on a pull block. Of course you would like to knock the man down if you can, but it is more important to be in control when you make contact. If you charge at the man out of control, it will be easy for him to sidestep you and make the tackle.

Once you've completed your assignment, you should try to block another man. Keep working until the whistle blows. When you look for another block, I recommend you simply hit the first defender you see. If you look around trying to figure out who's most likely to make the tackle, you may not hit anyone. My feeling is, the fewer guys chasing the runner, the better his chances of making more yardage.

On the cross block you will be blocking a man one position away from you. For example, say I'm to block the defensive end. That means the tackle will block my man, the defensive tackle. Or if I block the center's man, usually the middle linebacker, then the center will be blocking the defensive tackle.

Let me describe the play where the right guard switches with the right tackle. The job will be simply reversed with the center. First, the tackle will go ahead of you and hit your regular man. Your right foot should pivot about 45^0 and immediately after your tackle passes in front of you, fire out towards the defensive end.

This is not an easy block because as the defensive end reads the play he will want to pinch toward the middle to close the hole. Your block is to move him out. You should make contact off your right leg and then cut off the lane with your left step.

On the trap for Oakland, I was usually moving to the left side of the line to block either Art Shell's or Gene Upshaw's man. This time you pivot $90°$ on your left foot. Unlike the pull where you want to get in back of the offensive line about two yards, this time you want to stay directly on the line of scrimmage. As your teammates explode off the line, you're running right behind them, grazing their fannies.

As in the cross block, you want to block inside out in order to open the lane for the runner. Of course, the man you're blocking will try to pinch to close the hole. You explode off your left leg and protect with your right. So the blocking technique is basically the same as the pull or cross block.

You've already read John Hannah's explanation of the basic drive block and pass block. Let me just say some words about pass blocking. As a guard, your job is to keep the defensive tackle's penetration to less than three yards. That way, he can't get his hand up to block the passing lane. To do this, you must take your stand immediately. The offensive tackle can back off some because he is trying to work the defensive end toward the outside away from the quarterback.

Of course, everyone wants to know about the use of hands. There was a significant change in the rules concerning this before the 1978 season. We can now extend our arms more in order to absorb some of the blow.

When I pass block, I like to hit the man first with my helmet, right under his chin. I understand in many high schools that this is no longer legal, that blockers have to hit with their shoulders. That presents a problem because the easiest way around you is around your shoulder. You prefer to hit a defender in the middle of his chest.

Also new in the NFL is that we can hit with our open hand. If you're allowed to do this in your league, I recommend that as you bring your arms up to hit the defender you open your hands and hit with the heel of your palms. This is much easier on the hands than if you hit with the knuckles. But find out what the rules are in your league and obey them. You hurt the team if you're penalized for illegal use of the hands.

Pass blocking

The key word in pass protection is control. A lot of kids want to knock their man down and in trying to do so they get off balance and it's easy for their men to slip by. You must stay in control. You may have to give up a little of your power, but it is more important to stay in front of your man and control him. It is better to take short pops instead of lunging out. Make short, crisp blocks off one foot and then move the other foot to help keep you in front of your man.

Control is important in every block. It's a little like hitting a golf ball. If you swing too hard and try to kill it, you're most likely not going to hit it square. The same is true in blocking. It is more important to use your technique and keep control rather than trying to hit too hard.

In order to do this you must be in control of yourself on the football field. You have a specific job to do and you need a calm head to do it. If you allow yourself to become frustrated, you will have trouble maintaining your poise and you can hurt your team. Besides, frustration saps your strength. So it is important that you give your best on every play. If something goes wrong, learn from it, then forget it and move on to the next play.

Offensive Tackle
Jean Barrett
San Francisco 49ers

Jean Barrett gives the San Francisco 49ers a lot of flexibility on their offensive line. During his first six seasons, Jean started and played at center, guard and tackle. In 1976 he settled at left tackle, his favorite position.

Jean attended the University of Tulsa where he was a starter for three years and played in several all-star games following his senior year. An ankle injury against the Oakland Raiders forced him to sit out the 1978 season on the injured reserve list.

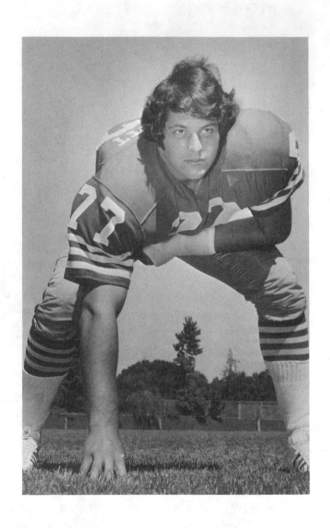

My height, 6' 6", along with my 248 pounds makes me ideally suited to play offensive tackle. I've played center and guard also, but in those positions it helps if you're a little shorter. The reason is leverage. If you are not taller than the defensive tackles you are blocking, it's easier to get underneath them on your blocks. And that's the key to being able to move them.

However, I'm glad I had the opportunity to play the other line positions. It gives me a better understanding of how to work with my teammates--the things they can do well and the things that are difficult for them. The basic skills as far as drive blocking, pass protection, setting up in a proper stance, are the same for center, guard, and tackle. But beyond that there are many subtle differences.

I feel the offensive guards are a little more confined than the tackles. As tackle I have a little more room to move around. Of course, the defensive end also has more room and if he's very quick, as many in the NFL are, you have to be careful. You can't deliver quite as strong a blow as the guard because the guard knows his man will be there on every play. If you overextend yourself with the defensive end, he is often agile enough to slip by you.

Therefore, I too have to use a word you've read several times already in this book—control. You must be in *control.* You can't overextend yourself. By that I mean you can't get your head out too far in front of your body. You need to keep your head up. You won't be able to hit quite as hard as if your head were out, but you'll be able to adjust to whatever the defensive end does.

Pass blocking is quite a bit different as far as strategy for an offensive tackle. The guard has less ground to protect because the defensive tackle is supposed to stay in his lane and the guard doesn't want to allow him much in the way of penetration. Also, if one of the defensive tackles is causing a lot of problems, the center can help out.

However, the offensive tackle is often split a little way from the guard, and he has more room to cover. The defensive end isn't as restricted in where he can go. But the tackle can use this extra room to his advantage by simply forcing him out of the play. By that I mean as he rushes up toward the quarterback, you can use his momentum to simply push him by the quarterback and out of the play.

You've already learned the stance and proper position for pass protection—the basic hitting position. So as I assume that position, I drop back about two or three feet off the line of scrimmage and wait. I keep my hands up for protection. There is a new rule in the NFL now, as George Buehler mentioned in the previous chapter, that allows us to hit with the palm of our hands, though a lot of lineman were doing that already.

What you want to do is mirror whatever the defensive end does. That way you keep between him and the quarterback. By doing that ultimately he has to try and go through you to reach his goal. When he does, you hit him using your arms and hands. You're actually trying to push him which accomplishes two things—it delays his charge and pushes you back so you can reset in your basic hitting position.

What ends up happening is you mirror, hit, recover, mirror, hit again, and so on until you're in position to finish the block. That's when he makes his final move toward the quarterback. If that move is upfield, you keep your head in front of your man, your forearm behind him, and you push him further upfield and out of play. If he decides to go inside, then to finish the block you alter your angle. You keep your head in front of him, but you push him into the congestion of the interior line and away from the quarterback. However, most defensive ends don't want to go inside because of that congestion. They'll try to play for the outside, looking for one or two times a game when they can fake you outside and blow past you inside.

So you must keep that in mind. You must never start anticipating his moves or you'll get beat. You must always mirror him. You're alone out there and there's no one to help you. If you're beat, the quarterback gets clobbered.

Because the defensive end has so much room to play with, you have to be careful. Some defensive ends will set up quite aways from the line and point at the quarterback. In this situation you don't want to get turned too much toward the sidelines. If you do it's easy for him to get by you.

Keep in mind that when the defensive end lines up that far out, he has a longer distance to travel to his target. He'll be coming out of a sprinters stance to get more speed, but he still has to go through you. Keep your position and meet him head on.

If he has trouble getting around you, the defensive end may try running over you and driving you into the quarterback. So you have to get low and drive underneath him. Another move he'll try is the swim in which he grabs one shoulder and pulls down, then uses his free hand to pull past you.

The key to defeating this move is to not let the man get a hold of you. You have to hit him as he grabs. If you time it right, his grab will come up empty handed. If he grabs you, then you need to get your arm in his arm pit and side and push. If you do that he can't pull your shoulder down and therefore he won't be able to get past you. In fact he's left his whole body exposed and you can put another good hit on him.

In summary, the basic moves you'll see a defensive end make on a pass rush are to go inside, outside, pull your shoulder, fake outside and go inside, and over you. His basic strategy is to get you off balance, to get your legs twisted so he can blow by you.

One other problem you may have on pass blocking is if the defensive tackle and defensive end crisscross. There are two ways to handle this. One is to area block and simply switch men. Then you use exactly the same blocking techniques as you would on the defensive end. The other is to man block. Here, you as the tackle stay with the defensive end while the guard drops back and waits for the defensive tackle to come around.

The decision as to which method to use should be decided before a game. The coaches will usually tell you what they want you to do. There's one thing you need to be aware of on this play. The defensive end may try to grab both the guard and tackle and thus free the defensive tackle for a clean break on the quarterback. You need to avoid this if at all possible.

An offensive tackle usually doesn't have to pull like a guard does. But there are a number of things he does that you should keep in mind. Many of them apply to all offensive linemen.

First is the double team block. We rarely do a pure double team in the pros. But you sometimes have to in lower levels because you may get a defensive lineman who is overpowering. The key on a double team block is for the two blockers to stay close together--you should actually be touching at the hips as you make contact with your opponent.

The main problem with double team blocks is that the defensive man can split through the two players if they aren't close together. So you should both aim to hit him in the center of his body. I think it is better on a double team for one guy to do most of the work as far as the drive block, and for the other to control, that is to see he doesn't slip away.

The more common situation in the pros is for two guys to double team block and then one blocker to slide off to block another man. On this double team, usually one man is responsible for about 90 percent of the block while the guy who slips off is responsible for about 10 percent. So the primary blocker should fire out and hit and the other player should control, to see he doesn't slip away, and then move to his other block.

A common play for me at tackle is hitting the defensive tackle and controlling him until the center can come over and block him after my guard pulls. Then I slide off and block the middle linebacker. Another situation develops when the outside linebacker is lined up between the defensive end and tackle. I start out blocking the defensive tackle and then slide off to block the linebacker. You'll learn more about these blocks as your coach teaches you plays for your team.

Here are a few other plays you'll have to be involved in. One is a play action pass. This is really one of the hardest blocks for a lineman to make. In order to make the quarterback's fake work, the other team has to really believe you are running. So you have to hit your man with a drive block. But you can't overextend yourself. You have to hit him with your head first, follow through with your hands and deliver a pop. This is how you push off him and drop into your pass protection stance.

The reason linemen are nervous about this play is, if you miss your man, the play is ruined. You're tempted to not hit your man on the drive block, but if you do that, the linebacker will immediately read the fake.

Another play is the draw. There are two kinds of draws —the middle and the outside. The middle is a fairly easy play. You simply drop into your normal pass protection position. But you slightly overplay the inside so the defensive end won't take that route. As he rushes upfield, you simply force him that way so he's out of the play. Then you can turn back upfield and block a linebacker or safety.

On the outside draw, the back will be going between you and the guard. You drop into your pass set and block as you do on pass protection. Again you want to force him upfield, only this time you stay with him until the play is over. The biggest problem on the draw happens when the defensive end gets inside. When he does the play is over and you probably will have a loss. So your job is to keep him from coming inside.

A third play is the screen and again there are two kinds— the quick and the regular delay. On the quick screen the offensive guard and tackle hit their men as they do on a play action. You want to drive block your men inside and this will force you outside. The quarterback will throw quick and you flow outside and hit whoever shows up.

On the regular screen you drop into your normal pass protection. You again mirror your man and stay in front of him for usually three counts. Then you do a cut or cross body block. The tackle wants to hit the defensive end so his hands at least hit the ground—that way he can't knock the pass down. Usually the guards and center will lead the blocking on the screen. They pass protect for two counts and then force their men inside and release outside.

This is about the only time I cut block. It's a risky play because you can miss him if you don't do it right. Usually you want to stay on your feet because you have a chance to accomplish more for your team. On the cut block, you should keep your head in front of your man, and when you throw your hip you should throw it about waist high. This will mean you'll get him about his knees. If you throw the block knee high, you'll hit him about the ankles, and it will be easy for him to jump over you.

The key to a good cut block is timing. If you think you're ready to make the block, wait and take one more step. You should aim for his waist and roll into him. I feel the best time to cut block is when you and the man are going across the field. It's hard for him to sidestep you then. But even then I still feel you're better off staying on your feet.

There is a great deal of difference between an offensive lineman and a defensive lineman. Sometimes on high school or junior high teams, you'll play both. But the offensive lineman has a lot to learn. It's not natural to come out of your stance. It's not natural to stay low. The defense has a lot of advantages because they can use their hands and don't have set plays like the offensive lineman.

So there is a lot of discipline and very little glory. They keep track of tackles, but nobody keeps track of the blocks you throw—except for the coaches that is. You may play well the whole game except one play when the man you're blocking breaks through and sacks the quarterback. Then you're the goat.

But you have to be dedicated to your job. You can't lose your temper or be very emotional. If you get beat stay with the basics and keep calm. You have to stay with your techniques or you'll get beat. The great offensive lines have great techniques and they never quit. They just keep working.

Personally, I don't see how you can have that control without Christ. For me He provides the motivation I need to keep that dedication and that emotional calm that you have to have to be a good lineman.

Catching The Football-Tight End
Charlie Sanders
Detroit Lions

After an outstanding career with the Detroit Lions, Charlie Sanders left professional football just prior to the 1978 season. In seven of his 10 seasons, he played in the Pro Bowl and was twice named all-pro tight end. He holds the all-time Lion record for pass catches with 336 during his career and he averaged 14.3 yards per catch while scoring 31 touchdowns.

Charlie was a physical phenomenon on the football field, playing with numerous aches and pains. He only missed 12 games because of injuries during his career. In 1977, he was permitted to use a computerized device called a TNS. The small unit was tucked in the back of his pants and connected to his legs with electrodes, allowing the pain impulses to his brain to be cut off from his tender hamstrings.

Charlie played college football and basketball at the University of Minnesota and was a star at both sports. He was drafted by the Lions in the third round in 1968.

It's rather amusing that I'm talking about how to catch a football because I've had to adopt some unorthodox methods. I lost two ligaments in my thumb and had to adjust my technique, especially on over the shoulder catches.

Regardless of your technique, however, there is one thing you as a receiver must always remember. Look at the ball and keep your eye on it. Concentrate on the ball. Never take your eye off of it until you've tucked it away.

Don't forget that point as I explain the techniques of catching a football. There are basically three hand positions you can use: one for below the waist, one for above your waist to the shoulders, and a third for over your shoulder.

When a ball is coming below your waist, you should have your hands open like a cup with the little fingers touching at the tip. The fingers should be pointing down slightly toward the ground.

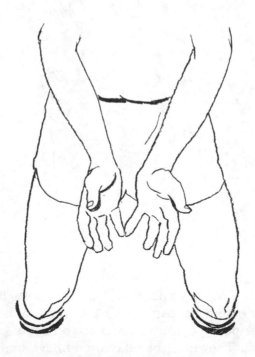

Catch below the waist

From the waist to the shoulders, you change your hand position, putting your thumbs together at their tips and holding your fingers up. The hands should be so positioned that the football will rest comfortably between them. This hand position is used on short and medium patterns.

When you are running deep and have to catch a ball over your shoulder, you should again position your hands with the small fingers touching. Only this time your fingers are facing straight up, rather than pointing toward the ground.

Catch from waist to shoulders

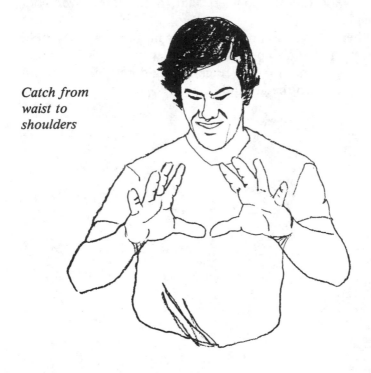

On all three of these positions, you must visually follow the ball into your hands. The nose of the football should fit into the position you've set. But you can't keep your hands rigid. They must be relaxed and have some give as the ball arrives.

Over the shoulder catch

This is especially important if you are catching from someone who throws the ball hard. You need more give in your hands then and you have to concentrate harder on the ball. Whatever you do, don't fight the ball. If the quarterback is throwing too hard, tell him to take a little off the ball.

After you catch the ball it is important that you always put it away. Tuck it in your arm like a runner does, with your hand covering the nose of the ball and the other end of the ball resting in the crook of your arm. Do this every single time you catch the ball. Raymond Berry did it even when he was playing a game of catch, so it became automatic.

Berry also practiced catching the ball every day. He used to say that if he didn't catch one hundred passes in a practice, he hadn't caught enough. I don't feel I need to catch that many, but I usually try to catch at least fifty passes every practice and I often stay after practice to work on my catching and pass patterns.

There is no substitute for practice in catching the ball. You need to continually keep at it. Beyond catching it, it is so important to know exactly where you are on the field. For example, on a throw over the middle, you need to catch the ball more with your body in order to protect it when you get hit.

That's probably the biggest problem young players have as receivers. They're afraid of being hit. If you are you shouldn't be a receiver, because you will get hit, especially as a tight end. He gets hit on every single play. You have to expect you will be hit and forget about it, because your job is to concentrate on catching the football. You can't do that if you're worrying about who's going to hit you.

Once you catch the ball and you have a chance to run with it, many young players make the mistake of running straight up and down. You must lean your body forward and bend your knees. You should read the chapter on running with the football and become used to holding the ball and running with it like the backs. If you run straight up and down you're going to get hurt. The secret to the longevity of men like Lydell Mitchell is that they almost never get hit by a solid straight-on shot.

Some people wonder when to begin looking for the ball on a pass pattern. I like to look as soon as I make my cut. That usually coincides with the time it takes the quarterback to drop back. If you look then you'll be ready if the quarterback has to throw in a hurry because of pressure.

When you catch the ball, meet it away from your body and draw it in. The reason for this is that it gives the defender a split second less time in which to try and knock the pass down. Often that split second means the difference between a reception and an incomplete pass.

You need to use your judgement as to when to leave your feet on a poor throw. Sometimes you'll need to stretch out to catch the ball. This requires great concentration because you can't take your eyes off the ball and expect to make the catch. Keep your same hand position when you do stretch out and watch the ball come into your hands. You have to concentrate hard to hold on to it because the ground will jolt you when you hit it. A lot of receivers lose these catches when they hit the ground.

A receiver should get to know his quarterback. The more you know him as a person, the better you'll understand how he thinks. And the more you work with him in practice, the better coordinated you'll be in a game. You should start working together long before training camp opens because it simply takes a lot of time to learn each other's moves and tendencies.

That's basically all there is to catching the football. Of course, I'm not explaining how to run pass patterns, etc. Steve Largent will do that for you. But let me take a moment to say a little about the tight end. In my opinion it is probably the most difficult position to play in football. That's because it is very demanding physically. You need the speed of a wide receiver, but you also need to block like a tackle. However, you have less weight than a tackle, and you frequently must give up a lot of weight on your blocking assignments.

A tight end is involved in every play, either blocking on the line or running a pass pattern. Sometimes you have to do both on the same play. A wide receiver has to block too, but not in the heart of the line like a tight end. So it is imperative that a tight end master the same blocking techniques as the other offensive linemen.

The pass patterns you run are basically the same as the wide receivers, though usually they will run theirs about five to ten yards deeper.

To be a tight end, you basically have to like football. You have to enjoy it and not consider it work. I never considered playing football a job. I know it's unusual for a tight end to hang around in the NFL as long as I did, but I think a big reason why I did is that I really enjoyed playing.

Whatever your position, you should enjoy playing too. You should enjoy becoming the best you can become. This will help your confidence and self concept, which is a big part of success in football. You have to believe you can do the job and do it well. When you do that you will find it very rewarding.

Wide Receiver
Steve Largent
Seattle Seahawks

Steve Largent surprised the National Football League in 1976 by finishing third among NFC receivers in his rookie season. The 5′ 11″ receiver caught 54 passes for 705 yards and four touchdowns with the expansion Seattle Seahawks. By 1979, he had established himself as one of the games premier receivers. He led the AFC in receiving in 1978, catching 71 passes for 1,168 yards and eight touchdowns. That won him a spot in the Pro Bowl, where he scored the only AFC touchdown.

Teamed with young quarterback Jim Zorn, this tandem has become one of the most exciting passing combinations in the league. In 1976 Steve was voted the Seahawks' offensive player of the year in a vote by local media. He was also voted the team's rookie of the year by local fans. In college he led the nation in touchdown catches in both 1974 and '75 while playing for Tulsa. In his final two years of school, he caught 103 passes for 1,884 yards and 28 touchdowns.

97

Ever since I've been in football, I've heard that in order to be a wide receiver you need to have speed and size. You need to be tall and be able to jump high. But that's simply not true and my being in the pros is proof. I'm only 5′ 11″ tall and I'm not going to burn any defenses with great speed.

I think the most important attribute of a good wide receiver is concentration. That's right—concentration. You have to be able to concentrate—that is to run perfect pass routes, to work with your quarterback on timing, and to "look" the ball into your hands on every pass.

Now if you do have speed, or height, or good hands, so much the better. These are all in your favor. But without concentration those advantages will be negated. Just remember all the world champion sprinters who couldn't make the pros as receivers. Compare them to players like Bob Berry and Danny Abramowicz. Neither of them were big and both were considered rather slow. However, Berry was one of the greatest pass receivers in NFL history, while Abramowicz, who was drafted by New Orleans in the 17th and final round, holds the NFL record for catching at least one pass in more than one hundred consecutive games.

One thing that has really helped me succeed in Seattle is working with our quarterback Jim Zorn. About two and a half months before training camp opens we start working out together. We spend hours working on our timing as I run pass patterns and he throws to me at the moment I make my cuts. By the time the season starts, we know each other so well and have practiced the plays so many times we could probably run some of them in our sleep.

You have already read what Charlie Sanders says about catching the football. Let me only reiterate that catching the ball requires that you watch the ball come into your hands. One little concentration drill I like is to notice where the laces are when the ball hits my hands. That way I know I'm watching the ball all the time. Remember that your first objective is to catch the ball. Only when you have caught it should you worry about running.

At the start of each play, it is important for you to have a proper stance, just as it is for the offensive linemen. In order to get a quicker jump off the line I recommend you use a three point stance. It is very important that you keep your head up. Don't look at the ground. One eye should be on your defender, the other eye on the ball. Because you are split away from the line, it is sometimes hard to hear the signals. You, therefore, need to watch for the snap in order to get a good jump.

Your release from the line of scrimmage should be the same on every play, run or pass—come off the ball hard with your head up. This prevents the defensive back from discovering the play before it develops. Practice running your patterns with your eyes focused on the defensive back, not on the point where you intend to cut. In this way your head fakes will be most effective.

Catching the ball is merely a part of a receiver's responsibility. His blocking also can play a key role in the running back's success. The technique I recommend is referred to as "shadow blocking." The object is to position your body between the defender and the running back, so as to force the defender to commit himself to one direction or the other. Once he has done this, force him further in that direction, allowing the running back to make the appropriate cut. Until the time the defender commits himself, a distance of one to two yards should be kept. Remember, many games have been won by long runs opened up by a receiver's block downfield.

Let's suppose the defensive man plays you right on the line. In this situation you must keep your head up, with your eyes on the defender. His intent is to destroy the timing of the play. So use a quick head and lateral step in one direction, then run the other. For a change-up use a double fake.

But if you are held up at the line, don't change your pass route. You must run exactly the same depth and make the cut exactly as planned. Many young players try to adjust when they are slowed down by a defender by making their cut a couple of yards short. It's not your job to adjust. A good quarterback will see your problem and adjust for you. The timing of the play is predicated on your making a specific move on a specific spot. Don't let anything keep you from doing that.

I would like to describe a few of the most common pass patterns receivers use. Most pass plays are run using these patterns or variations of them. However, the names will differ according to the team with which you play.

First is the post pattern. There is a deep post and a quick post, but the idea is basically the same. You come off the line of scrimmage with your eyes watching the defensive back. As you run aim for his inside shoulder. When you get to the depth where you are to make your break, give him a fake to his outside shoulder. This is done by making a stutter step move with your feet to the defender's outside.

The object here is to cause the defensive back to move toward the sideline, thinking that the pass is going that direction. Now you make your break, at about a 45⁰ angle to the center of the field. It's called a post because you are aiming for the goal posts as you run.

The next pass route is called the out or comeback. Here the idea is to make the defensive back think you are going deep. To do this you come off the line hard (you always go hard off the line) and run straight at the defensive back. Then as you near the defender, give him a quick fake inside. Continue upfield to the proper depth and cut outside and back toward the line of scrimmage at a 45° angle.

The curl route, or hook, is run identically to the comeback, with the difference being that the cut is made to the inside instead of the outside. The key in both patterns is to continue back until you've caught the ball. Never wait for the pass to come to you.

The last primary pattern is known by many names. I refer to it as the deep pattern. Come off the ball hard and go right at the defensive back. When you get on top of him, make a jab step to his inside shoulder causing him to think you're running a post pattern. Then burst straight up field keeping about five yards away from the sideline. This will allow for some degree of error in the quarterback's throw.

Most of the rest of the pass plays are run in combinations or variations of these four patterns. There are two mistakes that receivers often make in running patterns. The first is running out of control. By that I mean they run so fast that they can't make a quick break. It's not necessary to run at full speed as long as you make good sharp moves.

Second, many receivers become so concerned about running the perfect pattern that they forget to concentrate on catching the ball. Remember, that's your number one priority.

What do you do if you've run your pattern and the quarterback still has the ball? Perhaps he's scrambling because of a strong pass rush or all of his receivers were covered. When this happens it is most important that you move back towards the quarterback, not away from him. If you keep going deep you may run out of his throwing range, or more than likely out of his sight. He'll probably be looking short so run back toward the line of scrimmage, looking for an opening where there are no defenders. Do not wave your hands at the quarterback; if you're open, he'll find you. Keep moving, though, because if you stop the defense will cover you, making it difficult for the quarterback to get the ball to you.

Perhaps more than any other position, with the exception of quarterback, a wide receiver must keep his head. You can't lose your temper and expect to be effective as a receiver because most of your job is concentration. A defensive back will try to break your concentration, because if he does he's beaten you for the game. Therefore you have to forget about what he's doing and concentrate on your job.

One thing that helps me here is remembering that even if there are 60,000 people in the stands, I'm really only playing for an audience of one. And that person is my

Lord Jesus Christ. He's the One I want to please and I can do that by playing to my utmost. If I do my best I don't have to compare myself to anyone else because I know I'm a winner in God's eyes.

Quarterback
Jim Zorn
Seattle Seahawks

The Seattle Seahawks in their first three seasons in the NFL have set a new standard of excellence for expansion teams. And quarterback Jim Zorn is one of the primary reasons why the club set records for victories in both their second (five) and third seasons (nine). In 1978, they twice defeated the powerful Oakland Raiders and came within one win of making the playoffs.

In 1978, the left-hander was third in the NFL in yardage gained by passing. He completed 248 passes for 3,283 yards and 15 touchdowns. In his rookie season, Zorn led the NFL with 439 passing attempts, completing 208. He set NFL records for passing yardage (2,571) both as a rookie and an expansion quarterback. An injury caused him to miss four games in 1977, but he still managed to complete 104 passes for 1,687 yards and 16 touchdowns.

Jim was signed as a free agent by the Dallas Cowboys in 1975 after a college career at Cal Poly (Pomona). The Cowboys made Zorn their final cut in '75 to make room for Preston Pearson. Zorn then signed as a free agent with the Seahawks. Following his outstanding rookie season, he was voted the NFC Offensive Rookie of the Year by the NFL Players Association.

Some people still think all you need to be a good quarterback is a strong, accurate arm. That's simply not true. If you have dreams of being a successful quarterback, you need to be an all-round, well-conditioned athlete.

When I train during the off season, I probably lift as many weights as any other ball player. Though I'm not lifting to put on bulk, I'm not afraid to lift heavy weights in order to build up strength. I don't say that every quarterback should do what I do. I do think, however, a good all-round conditioning program will pay off in your ability to perform on the football field, in lessening the risk of injury and, if you are injured, in speeding your recovery.

When I tore a ligament in my left leg in 1977, I only missed four games. I'm convinced that was because I was in good shape. The muscles around that ligament were

strong and so it healed quickly. I'm glad because in my first game back, we beat Buffalo 56-17 for our greatest win up to that point.

There are so many things a quarterback must do on the football field. Craig Morton has already given you some of the basics of throwing a pass. That's only a part of it though and I'd like to briefly review some of the other essentials for being a good field general. We can't go into great depth, but I can give you some basics.

Three ways to take a snap

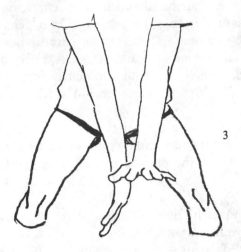

3

The first thing you must do is take the snap from the center. When I walk to the line of scrimmage after calling a play in the huddle, I'm looking over the defense to decide whether the play I called is going to work, or if I need to call an audible. Therefore, the last thing I need is to be worrying about the snap. It should be automatic by the time I get into a game. However, it takes a lot of practice with your center to get to that point.

There are three generally accepted ways for a quarterback to take a snap: 1) with his hands one on top of the other, touching at the heel of the palm, in a V-shape; 2) with both hands facing toward the ground, touching at the thumbs, resting on the roof of the center's rear; and 3) with one hand on the roof of the center's rear and the other, touching at the thumbs, angled down at 90⁰ toward the ground.

I prefer the third way myself. The first way, your right arm (though I'm left handed, I'll write this for a right hander) will be cramped and so far under the center it becomes awkward. The second way I feel is the riskiest as far as a possible fumble. The third method is the most comfortable for me. When the ball hits your upper hand, the other hand very naturally closes around the ball.

When you put your hands under the center, he should feel some pressure from your top hand in order to know where to put the ball. However, be careful not to put too much pressure. One of our centers has a very balanced stance and sometimes, if I put too much pressure under him, it upsets his timing; you need to work this out together.

The snap should come with the laces facing into the fingers of your passing hand. You should never have to worry about where the laces are. This way, you can always be ready to pass, handoff, pitch or run with the football.

When you take the handoff *always,* repeat *always pull the ball into your stomach or chest.* This is a key to good ball handling. If your arms are extended, it's very easy for a defensive man to knock it out of your hands. When the ball is in your stomach there's less chance of fumble,

Always pull the ball into your stomach or chest

The handoff

and it's harder for the defense to see what you're doing with it.

When you pull the ball in after the snap, you are in proper position to make a handoff. At this point a caution— *do not false step*. Many young quarterbacks jab step, or hesitate, or make a false step of some sort. That slows you down and timing is so crucial to successful offense. So you must know exactly what your footwork is before each play starts and this comes through practice.

As you step toward the ball carrier there are three ways you can give him the ball: 1) you can place it with one hand; 2) you can place it with two hands; or 3) you can place it with two hands and pull one hand. The third one is effective if you want to fake the linebacker into thinking you may be keeping the ball. I always start the ball into the running back's gut with both of my hands, in order to insure control.

When you make a handoff you must watch the ball as it moves into the runner's stomach. When I fumble on an exchange it's almost always because I didn't "look" the ball into the runner's stomach. Even if you're faking and will take the ball back, "look" it into the runner's pocket.

Your job is not finished once you've handed off to a running back. In fact it's just beginning. You must make a fake. You must do something on every play after you hand off the ball. The one thing you must *not* do is watch the runner. Instead, look over the defense to see how they're reacting to the play. You have to be an actor on the field, a magician. A good offense causes a moment's hesitation among the linebackers and defensive backs that can mean the difference between a decent gain or no gain.

The key is your consistent faking. After the handoff you can fake a bootleg and run outside, or you can drop back like you're going to pass, depending upon what your coach wants you to do. Then when you do fake a run and bootleg or drop back to throw, you've created a moment's hesitation on the defense. They don't know for sure if the runner has the ball. They may even tackle the "ball carrier" and that can give you valuable extra time.

If you are faking the handoff you can either put the ball in the back's stomach and pull it away, or you can put a hand in and keep the ball on your hip. In either case look into his stomach as you do on an actual handoff.

Another important thing to keep in mind on handoffs: don't turn your back on the line of scrimmage. Many quarterbacks make this mistake. Except on a bootleg, or occasionally on other plays, you should always face downfield. Even on passes, you should work on getting back without turning around. This way you can always be analyzing the other team and seeing how they react or watching your receivers and how they're working.

Two effective plays being used today on all levels of football are the option and the sprint out. On both of these plays the quarterback needs speed and quickness. You move down the line of scrimmage on the basic option play. Your tackle will not block the defensive end, and what you do depends on how the defensive end reacts. If you run the play well the defensive end has to decide whether to go after you or cover the running back who's trailing. If he goes to tackle you, you pitch to the running back. If he covers the back, you go inside and keep the ball.

113

In the pros we don't run this play often because it's rough on the quarterback. We don't wear as much in the way of protection as the other players, so it is more dangerous.

A play we prefer to run is the sprint out. This is an option to run or pass. It is a great play to use if you have the speed necessary to get outside quickly. On the snap you run back about seven yards at a 45° angle into the backfield and then cut upfield toward the sideline at another 45° angle. Now you're putting pressure on the defensive backs and linebackers. They have to decide whether to cover the ends close or move up to cover your run. If they move up or hesitate, you throw. If they drop back to cover the pass, you run with the ball.

One thing to keep in mind when throwing on the run is that you don't need as much power on the ball because you have more momentum. When you throw, instead of leading the receiver (on a sideline pass), you should throw straight at him. Your momentum will cause the pass to go wide, and so will naturally lead the receiver. However, you must practice this as it requires timing.

Of course all of what I'm explaining requires practice. There's no easy way. In the off season you should work as often as possible with your ends and backs, doing pass patterns and various other plays. About two or three months before the Seahawks open their training camp, I'm working several times a week with Steve Largent and the other Seattle receivers.

Some other things to keep in mind are as follows. Don't worry about the defensive pressure, especially when you're attempting to pass. If you do your job and you get sacked, it's not your fault. Too many young quarterbacks leave their protective pocket too soon because of the pressure. If you do that and you get sacked, that is your fault. You need to drop back, look for your receivers and throw. You don't have time to be worrying about the defensive line.

What if a teammate makes a mistake? Say one of your ends drops the ball. I'll tell you what you'd better *not* do. That's yell at him. If you get on a guy for dropping a pass, he will lose his respect for you. Your job is to give one hundred percent. If your teammates see you doing your best, then they'll try their best. If they make a mistake just think of the times you overthrew a receiver or made some other error. Encourage your receivers and your teammates. Your job is not to yell at them, but to encourage them. Leave the criticism to the coaches.

As far as leadership goes, every quarterback has his own style. Some are "rah, rah" cheerleaders. Some are quiet. Some are very serious. Any type is all right as long as you are being yourself. If you try to be "rah, rah" when you're naturally quiet, then your teammates will see it as a fraud. My style is to encourage the guys as much as I can.

Remember that you're in charge on the field. There should be no talking in the huddle. You're in command. If there is a problem, delegate responsibility to your center to make sure everyone is quiet before you step into the huddle. If anyone has a suggestion the time to make it is on the sideline between series, or occasionally between plays—but *never* in the huddle.

If you want to be a good quarterback, you have to work hard and you need to be prepared. There are so many things we don't have room to talk about, but when you practice your coach will help you learn what to do in different situations, what plays to call, how to give audible signals, etc.

I want to emphasize the importance of preparation. You need to be prepared physically, and that includes a proper off season conditioning program, as well as working on your basic skills. Second, you need to be prepared mentally. That's what you do each week in practice before a game, learning what the other team does, and what plays to call, etc. Third, you need to be prepared emotionally. You can't get upset on the field, or get rattled by defensive pressure.

The most important form of preparation, however, and the one I believe sets the tone for the other three areas, is spiritual. You must prepare spiritually. The way you do that is by having a clear conscience. The only way I know to have a clear conscience is by accepting Jesus Christ. He is the One who paid the penalty for our sins by dying on the cross. He gives us a new life through His ressurection. We are completely freed from the guilt of sin if we accept Christ. For me that is the starting point in my preparation to play football, or in anything else I do.

My goal in football is not to be famous, or make a lot of money, but to glorify God. By that, I mean that God has given me my abilities and I must develop them to their full potential and do my best to please Him. In that way I fulfill God's plan for me. When I do this I don't need to be embarrassed or ashamed about what happens on the field.

Running Back
Robert Miller
Minnesota Vikings

Chuck Foreman receives a lot of the glory on the Minnesota Vikings for his 1,000 yard rushing seasons. But one man who helps him gain those yards is Robert Miller. The Kansas graduate is "exhibit A" that a running back not only runs with the football, but makes a valuable team contribution as a blocker and pass receiver.

Miller is not big as far as backs go, standing only 5′ 11″ tall and weighing 210 pounds. In 1976 he gained 286 yards rushing, and caught 23 passes for 181 yards. In 1977 he gained more yards as a receiver (246) than he did as a runner.

117

Running back is an ego-centered position. Every back would like to think he could carry the ball every play. He's an eternal optimist. He thinks the next time he carries the ball, he's going to score. The problem with this is that you can't have that kind of a selfish attitude on a football team.

That's especially true in my position on the Vikings. Chuck's job is to run with the football. My job is to block on many of the plays. Of course I'm confident I can perform when called upon to run with the football, but I'm also satisfied doing my job as a blocker.

That's a very important point for all running backs to keep in mind. A great back is not just a great runner. He's an all-round football player. He can block, carry out fakes, pass protect, run pass patterns and catch passes. It is also beneficial if he can throw a pass now and then. The point is, if you want to be a running back, you need to develop your total skills, and that involves a lot more than just running with the football.

You don't have to be big to be effective as a blocker. I'm only 5′ 11″ and 210 pounds, which is small for the NFL. I've had to block guys like Ed "Too Tall" Jones who's 6′ 9″ and 265 pounds. I'm not going to overpower him so I have to use my head and I have to play smart. Doing that has helped me survive four seasons.

Blocking as a back is different than blocking on the line. On the line of scrimmage you're going to make contact immediately. As a back you either have to run a few yards to make your block, or you have a longer wait on pass protection. Because of this, while the principles of blocking are the same, some of the techniques are different.

For example, on pass protection you set up in the basic hitting position the same way an offensive lineman does. But when the man you're blocking comes within striking distance, there are three ways you can handle him. First, you can explode through his numbers, and like the linemen, back up after the hit and do it again.

If the man is much bigger than you, you can't keep this up because he'll overpower you. So another method is that when the defender comes within striking distance, you explode and hit him at the thighs, driving your shoulders through his thighs. Do that once or twice and your man will be thinking twice when he comes into the backfield again.

A third maneuver is, as the defender comes within striking distance, open up the outside lane to the quarterback by stepping toward the inside with your inside foot and back with your outside foot. To do this, as well as the others blocks, you should always keep in mind where your quarterback is and keep between him and the man you're blocking. When you open up the lane to the quarterback, the defender will of course forget about you and think only about the sack. As he reaches the spot opposite the middle of your chest, you explode out of your basic position and hit him in his ribs. Using his momentum against him you ride him out of the play much as a tackle rides a defensive end out of the play on pass protection.

Blocking on pass rush

When you're blocking for a running play, it helps to know the style of the back you're blocking for. With Chuck Foreman it doesn't take much room for him to move. That makes my job easier. Most of the time my assignment is to block a linebacker—I'd say about eighty-five percent of the time. The key to successful blocks on a running play is to stay low. As you come out of your stance, don't stand completely up. Keep low and hit your man with a basic shoulder block.

What you want to accomplish is to open a lane for your runner. That means you want to block a man either inside out or outside in. To do this you should hit the man in the numbers and drive him in the appropriate direction, while moving your body to shield the runner from the would-be tackler.

For example, say the play is a sweep right. Chuck Foreman is running about an arm's length behind me. As I prepare to hit the defender, I want to drive him to the right, toward the sideline so Chuck can go inside. I hit him with a right shoulder and swing my body around to the left so I'm driving him toward the sideline. Chuck will then go right behind me, toward my left to take advantage of the block. That's the basic idea on all the blocks you use for running plays.

Another important part of being a back is carrying out effective fakes. If the quarterback fakes a handoff to you, you need to run exactly as if you had the ball. Someone ought to hit you if you're doing your job. A lot of ball players don't like this. They don't want to be hit unless they have to be.

If you let up though and don't get hit by the defense, then your team's fake won't do much, if any, good. So you must go full speed, and if no one hits you, you'll be open for a pass. This is very important to the success of your team.

With Minnesota, the backs run a lot of pass patterns and catch a lot of passes. Foreman and I together caught more passes than any wide receiver in the NFL in 1977. Usually these passes are short swing passes or passes in the flat. We run basically the same patterns as a receiver, but we don't run them as deep.

Often we have a play where I stay back to block a linebacker if he rushes. If he doesn't rush then I go out on a pass pattern and try to draw the linebacker. If he stays back to help cover a receiver, I'll be open. If he comes up to cover me, it makes it easier for a receiver to get open.

Playing with Minnesota I've had to get used to playing in less than ideal conditions. Perhaps you saw us play the Rams in the mud in the 1977 playoffs or have seen us in the cold, icy conditions in Minnesota. If you have to play on muddy or icy fields, you need to adjust your footwork in order to stay on your feet.

Personally, on a bad field, I like to use the three point staggered stance. I've studied the great runners like Gale Sayers and Jim Brown. On a dry field they would run on the balls of their feet, but in poor conditions they were able to maintain their effectiveness by running flat-footed. I've found that makes a big difference because if you're flat-footed, you have more control and can change direction easier than if you're on your toes.

That's an example of how you can learn from watching great players. However, let me warn you about what not to do—don't copy another player's style. Today, everyone wants to run like O.J. Simpson or Walter Payton. When I was a kid everyone wanted to play like Johnny Unitas. The problem is you don't have the exact same skills as Simpson or Payton or Unitas. *I believe you should work to develop your own talents and skills.* No one is made exactly the same, so except for learning techniques from other players, you shouldn't copy someone else.

Another problem young football players have is they start out with the wrong attitude. A running back is not the whole team. Football is a team sport. It takes eleven players on offense and eleven on defense, as well as special teams in order to win. So a back needs to sacrifice for the good of the whole team. Sometimes that means you won't gain as many yards as you would like or think you can.

That's not easy. Even older backs have to battle this problem. But when I have a selfish attitude, I ask God to forgive me and remember that God gave me the ability to play ball and He put me in the position I am in. He doesn't want me to sulk because I'm not running the ball much. He wants me to glorify Him by doing my best on every play, whether it's blocking, running or catching the ball.

Tackling
Jeff Siemon
Minnesota Vikings

Jeff Siemon saves some of his best games for national television. As middle linebacker for Stanford University, he helped his school win two consecutive Rose Bowl games in upsets over Ohio State and Michigan. And in Super Bowl XI he was one of the few bright spots for the Minnesota Vikings as he made fifteen unassisted tackles against the Oakland Raiders.

When Lonnie Warwick was injured in 1972, Siemon the rookie stepped into the starting middle linebacker spot and has been there ever since. Four times in his first six seasons, he was named to the NFC Pro Bowl squad. In 1976 Jeff led the Vikings in tackles with 146, plus 42 assists. He was also credited with causing two fumbles and blocking a field goal. In six seasons he's intercepted eleven passes, returning them for 104 yards.

You only have to look at the championship teams in the NFL to understand what ultimately wins football games. It's defense. Almost always, the eight playoff teams will be among the top ten defensive teams in the league. A strong defense can often carry a weak offense. But a strong offense coupled with a weak defense will have a tough time winning the big games.

The secret to Minnesota being at or near the top of the league year after year is our defense. There are three things that characterize the personnel on our squad, or any good defense. The first two go together: aggressiveness and instinct. On offense you can be a little more thoughtful, more precise and methodical; but on defense, you need a degree of recklessness.

But there is a third requirement—discipline. Everyone on the Minnesota defense has a job to do. When everyone does his job, we win. Generally, when I make a mistake it's because I try to do something above and beyond my responsibility, before I've completed my assignment.

I've seen many great physical specimens come into training camp. They had great talent and were aggressive. They didn't make the team, however, because they lacked discipline. There are some truly great athletes who have even achieved notoriety as linebackers by making spectacular plays; but they also fail to make plays because they are so frequently out of position. The teams they play for aren't among the winners in the NFL.

So while it is important to be aggressive and have a nose for the football, you must be disciplined. You must do the job your coach wants you to do. Once you've done your assignment, of course, you must pursue. You'll see that word a lot in this book because you want a defense in which everyone is pursuing the ball carrier. But that comes only after you've checked your area of responsibility.

The number one objective of the defense is to get the ball back for the offense. This may mean making them punt, or better yet causing a fumble or interception. The more your offense is on the field the better your chances of victory. Your second objective is not to just

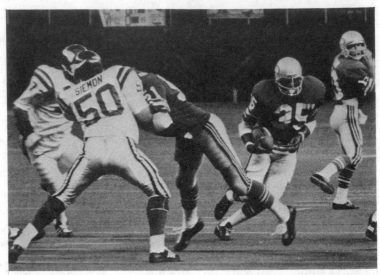

give the offense the ball, but to give it to them in good field position.

In order to achieve these objectives, most of the time the defense wants to make the offense throw the ball. Usually the offense prefers to run because there is less risk. If they can make five yards a play by running, they'll control the game. With a pass there is the risk of an interception, or a sack of the quarterback for the big loss. However, with a team like Oakland in the NFL, I don't think a team gains anything by making them pass. But with most teams you do. Even Oakland would prefer to establish their running game in order to make their passing more effective.

The most important technique on defense is tackling. There are two basic tackles we practice with the Vikings. One is the head on, perfect form tackle. The other is the angle tackle where the ball carrier is running by you. There are variations of each, but if you practice these two, you'll be in good shape. You rarely make a perfect form tackle in a game, but the principles are always used.

Let me first explain the head on tackle. You want your head up and your face mask in the runner's numbers. Your knees and hips are flexed. This is the basic hitting position John Hannah described. When you make contact you wrap your arms around the ball carrier and your legs explode up through him. The crucial ingredient is the wrapping of your arms. Today running backs are so big and strong and fast that just a good solid hit probably won't knock them off their feet, so you must get your arms around them.

The angle tackle is used when a man is running by you. Let me explain it with the runner going by on your right. First, you must always keep your head in front of the man you're tackling. You throw your right arm into his numbers and the left arm follows behind him with a wrap. On this tackle the running back will usually fall forward, or at least sideways.

As with the head on tackle, your knees are bent, your head is up and you must get good extension of your hips and legs through the man. By keeping your head in front of the runner, you meet his force with yours.

Head on tackle

Head on tackle

There are ideal forms of course. In an actual game you want to get the runner down any way you can. Sometimes you have to lunge and grab an ankle or a shirt; you hold on to anything you can. Even if you just slow him down, you can usually get help.

That's why gang tackling is so important. In the NFL a tackler can't always bring backs down one on one because they're so good. Someone usually makes the initial hit and others help. You want to get into the habit of helping your teammates so you should try to be a part of as many tackles as you can.

The purpose of gang tackling is to keep the runner from falling forward. You want to put him on his back. A runner can gain a few more yards just falling forward. Even in gang tackling though, remember to always wrap your arms.

Angle tackle

I was reminded of this when in 1975 I came in to help tackle Larry Schreiber in a game against the 49ers. I didn't wrap my arms; instead, my hit helped him to regain his balance and go forward for several more yards and a crucial first down. I've seen it happen so many times. If you don't wrap your arms, a good hit may only allow the runner to regain his balance and gain more yardage.

There is a third form of tackle that I do not recommend for young ball players. That's what is called a cut tackle. Defensive backs like to use this when they are trying to tackle someone considerably heavier and stronger than they are. The defender throws his body at the knees of the running back and tries to cut his legs out from under him. They like this because there isn't as much shock on the body.

But the problem with this tackle is that there is a lot

131

of risk. If it works, the back will go down immediately but if you miss and he sidesteps you, he may break for a big gain. It's an all or nothing tackle. It looks spectacular if you make it. But it's also easy to miss completely.

I recommend, even with a mismatch, that you use the basic form tackle with the head up looking at the numbers and your arms wrapped around the ball carrier. In this way you can at least slow him down so help can come. Usually on a mismatch it's the defensive back making the play and he's the last line of defense. If you don't stop him, he'll score. The form tackle gives you a better chance to prevent the score.

Another tackle is the sideline tackle. There is some skill to this, especially with a fast ball carrier. You want to use the sideline as an extra defender. The ball carrier doesn't want to go out of bounds, so he's hemmed in. As you pursue you want to cut off his inside move. This is the one time you tackle with your head behind the ball carrier instead of in front. Your lead arm is in his numbers and the other arm wraps as with the angle tackle; you want to pull him out of bounds. The angle is key here. You want to take a proper angle so that he can't fake you and cut back inside.

There are three basic mistakes made in tackling. The worst mistake is keeping your head down. It is the number one way in which you can get seriously hurt playing football. Never forget this: *if you keep your head up, you won't get hurt.* A friend of mine in high school named Bob Simmons forgot this when he was playing freshman ball at the University of California, Berkeley. He was playing Stanford, where I went to school, and he had his head down on a tackle and broke his neck. He died a few hours later.

When you make a hit with your head down, you put tremendous pressure on your spinal cord. Also, of course, you can't see the runner if he makes a last-second move on you, and you may miss him completely.

The second mistake is not wrapping your arms. If you simply try to knock a guy off his feet, you may make a

132

couple of spectacular plays, but you'll miss more often than not and hurt your team. So always wrap your arms.

The third mistake is lunging at a player. When you do that you don't generate enough force to make a tackle. The key to a good tackle is uncoiling, with the power coming through your legs. If you lunge, you've lost that power. Save your uncoiling until you are only a couple of feet from the ball carrier.

Before you can make a tackle, you need to be able to avoid and/or defeat blocks. This is especially crucial for linebackers because you're being blocked on every play. Tackling is probably the easiest job for a linebacker and the most fun, but you can't make the tackle without beating your blocker.

There are two ways to do this. The first is to meet the blocker with force. You always use this on the line when a blocker is coming straight at you and the ball is coming toward you. You want to use your forearm or shoulder and deliver your blow under his shoulder pads. You bend your legs and thrust your hips—uncoil—in order to neutralize his charge. Then you use your hands to get rid of him and find the runner.

The other means of avoiding the block is used when pursuing or when the ball is going away from you. Here, you are eager to get to the ball carrier as quickly as possible, so you do anything you can to get to him, even leaping over a blocker. Here you use your agility and quickness, head fakes, whatever is necessary to avoid the block or minimize the time getting to the ball.

Defense is a difficult job and requires a lot of skill and study. Basically, while your team is eleven guys playing eleven guys, it breaks down to eleven games of one on one. You have to beat your man. To do so you need good technique, and you need enthusiasm and aggressiveness; they go hand in hand. There are different expressions of enthusiasm. They take different forms based on a player's personality. But if you play enthusiastically, it rubs off.

The way I try to maintain my enthusiasm is to remember who I'm representing on the football field—Jesus Christ.

There is a spiritual incentive for me to do my best, to give everything I can to play to my maximum potential. I see many great athletes come into camp every year and not make the team because they have attitude problems. Since ability is pretty even in the NFL, it's generally attitude that sets the great athletes apart. I believe playing for Christ allows me to maintain a proper positive attitude.

Defensive Tackle
Mike McCoy
Oakland Raiders

Mike McCoy had his big moment in the spotlight on January 1, 1978 as he picked up a fumble by the Denver Broncos and raced down the sideline towards an apparent touchdown. Unfortunately, the referees didn't see the fumble and ruled the play dead. Instead of an Oakland touchdown, Denver had the ball two yards away from the goal line. They quickly scored and went on to win the AFC championship.

After seven years with the Green Bay Packers, McCoy had to learn a new position as he was traded to Oakland for a first round draft choice in the pre-season. As part of a 3-4 defense, Mike was installed as middle guard behind starter Dave Rowe. With the Pack, Mike was a regular at defensive tackle since the opening game of his rookie season in 1970. He had played 82 consecutive games prior to the 1978 season.

In 1976 Mike led the Packer front four in nearly every major defensive category, including solo tackles (74), assists (16) and fumble recoveries (3). He also tied for the lead in quarterback sacks with 8½. McCoy is considered one of the best in pro football in defending against the run. During his college career he was chosen all-American by consensus at Notre Dame and was the second player chosen in the 1970 draft behind only Terry Bradshaw. McCoy stands 6' 5" tall and weighs 280 pounds.

It was very obvious because of my fast growth that I'd be a lineman if I played football. I was 150 pounds in the third grade, and by the time I was old enough to play in junior football programs, I weighed over 180 pounds. The mothers took one look at me and decided I wasn't going to play against their boys, so I was banned from the league. Consequently I didn't start in football until I was a sophomore in high school.

Almost everyone wants to play the "glamour" positions in football—quarterback, running back and wide receiver. You don't see many people volunteering, initially, to play offensive or defensive line. I'd encourage everyone to try his favorite position and find out if he is able to play there. If not, try something else.

Because of my size I was destined to be a lineman. But you don't have to be that big to play the line in Pop Warner or junior high ball. In high school you can put on weight through lifting. But don't start weight training until your advisor (parents, coach, doctor) say you are physically able. Then do it under supervision and on a carefully planned program. If you work at it, incorporating good eating and nutrition, you can put on the additional weight necessary to perhaps play college ball.

There are different philosophies of defense and what I say must be incorporated into what your coach wants you to do. Some coaches like a player to fire off the line and attack. Others want you to read and react. Your job will vary according to whether you play a 4-3, 3-4, 5-2, etc. Most of my career I've been a defensive tackle, but in 1977 I was traded to Oakland and had to learn a new position as middle guard.

My job with Oakland is to tie up the middle. If I can keep the guards and center off the linebackers, the other team won't gain much running up the middle. In passing situations they don't want me penetrating too deep. They want the center lane clogged so the quarterback can't run up the middle, and if I can knock down a pass or two, all the better. So you don't necessarily have to make the sack in order to be doing your job.

What you'll do will vary according to the philosophy of your coach. In Pop Warner leagues I wouldn't be too concerned about size and speed. You need to work on the fundamentals. First you must develop a good stance.

For a proper stance you should keep these elements in mind. Start with your feel parallel to each other and perpendicular to the line of scrimmage. Then if you are right-handed, put your right foot back until your right toe is even with your left heel. (Do the opposite if you're left-handed.) Then place both of your elbows on your knees. Let your right hand go forward until it touches the ground and leave your left elbow on your knee.

This will put you in the proper stance. Your weight should be in the middle of your body so if someone were to push you from any direction, you'd still keep your balance. You can put a little weight on your right hand, but not too much.

It is a big help if you get to know the cadence of the quarterback you're playing against. It will help you get a quicker jump, and that's so important to your success. In high school it's usually pretty easy to learn the cadence. A quarterback will usually go on a quick count, or the first, second or third "hutt." You don't guess, but you learn what he does in different situations and begin to anticipate it.

As soon as the football is moving, you want to be moving. If you wait to move until the quarterback has the ball, you're too late. Learn to move as soon as the center moves the ball. That means you should be looking at the ball with one eye. That's not too difficult for a defensive tackle, and for a middle guard it's easy since you're right over the center.

The first thing you want to do on the snap is neutralize your blocker. The best way to do that is, as soon as you make contact, throw your forearm. Learn to use that right forearm you have (left if you're left-handed). It's a great weapon and it can keep your blocker off balance. You also have the right to use your hands and you should take advantage of that.

Neutralize blocker
with forearm

Unlike the offensive lineman who makes a short step before making contact, you want to make contact with your opponent as you complete your first step. Then use your forearm on his head or catch him with your shoulder and biceps under his chin. You want to get under him and stand him up.

Once you've done this, look for the ball carrier and react. Your left arm should be free to push off or do whatever is necessary to shake the blocker.

You can usually tell what the play will be by what the guard does. If he drives straight ahead, it's probably a power play or a dive. If he hooks you, the play will probably be outside. Of course if he drops back into pass protection, you know it's a pass.

In high school and junior high ball, you can often pick up more tips about the play before the snap. For example, the guard may place extra weight on his hand before a drive block and shift that weight to his legs for a pass. He may move his foot or his eyes a certain way if he's going to pull. Any little tip you can pick up like this will help you gain an advantage in stopping the play.

Jeff Siemon has already told you how to make a tackle, so I won't go into any more about covering the run. If the blocker in front of you drops into pass protection, then you have a different objective. Rather than trying to neutralize him, you want instead to take a side. He'll be trying to hit you in the chest. You have a better chance to get by if you can get to one side of him.

The key to rushing the passer is getting a jump on your blocker. You can try to blow a gap, or fake him outside and go inside. The key is to keep the blocker away from you so you can maneuver. You want to get him to move one way while you're going the other. Remember you'll never be able to run over a guy, but you can usually beat him on one side.

Remember too, you can use your hands. One good move to learn is to grab the blocker on one side of his shoulder pads and jerk his shoulder down. Then take your other hand in a swim technique and pull on the

Swim technique

141

back of his jersey as you pass him. The feet are important on this move. You meet the guy with your feet square and when you jerk down (let's say you're using your right hand to jerk down his left shoulder) then your left foot starts coming inside. As you move your left foot, your left hand comes over his right shoulder. As you push off with your left hand, you're by him and heading for the quarterback.

Sometimes in the middle you'll be double teamed, so it will be physically demanding. If you're playing middle guard you'll most certainly be double teamed by the center and one of the guards. The center is easy to beat because his hands are between his legs. You simply need to get the jump as he starts the snap.

There are many variations on these basics, but they're too complicated to go into here. You can switch with the defensive end and let him charge inside while you go outside, or you can switch with a linebacker to try to confuse the other team's blocking.

The key to a successful defense is pursuit. You're not going to make the tackle on the line of scrimmage every play, so you have to be willing to pursue the runner. If the play is away from you, move down the line of scrimmage to get the right angle on the runner. Proper angles are everything here. No matter how fast the runner is, if you have the right angle on him, you can meet him.

Because of the angles, I don't recommend you run around the blocks. I suggest you fight them so you can keep your proper pursuit angles. Also, if you try to avoid the block, you may make a big play once in a while, but they can also take advantage of that to pull you out of position and run by you for a big gain. I suggest, therefore, you learn to fight off and break blocks.

The key to breaking blocks is staying low. If a blocker drives under you, you must get lower. Try to take away his advantage. If I am square I can dip my shoulder, turn the upper part of my body and spin by him, or I can meet him with my hands and ward him off.

The biggest mistake young players make on the line is standing up and looking around. When they do that it's easy for blockers to control them. If you stand up you've lost that play. The best way to play is to fire out of your stance with your back parallel to the ground. The important thing is to play the man in front of you. Don't worry about any fakes in the backfield. They shouldn't affect you.

One other thing I should mention is what to do on goal

line stands. You've got to say low. If you stand up they'll drive you back and score easily. Get low and make some penetration. Then the linebackers will be responsible for the tackle. In goal line or short yardage situations, I get in a four point stance in order to get more power in my drive off the line. All my weight is forward and I drive for the blocker's knees.

If you like playing football, you should do whatever is necessary to become as good as you can at your position. It requires a lot of work and a lot of training. You have to be aggressive on the defensive line. You have to develop a hunger to be around the football. One of the biggest mistakes young players make is they don't go after the football. That's your purpose on defense. You should make it a contest to see who gets to the football first.

If you'll be aggressive and determined to be where the football is, and if you're prepared physically, mentally and spiritually, you should be able to go hard on every down. Most fatique is mental. You really don't know what your body can do. When we played Baltimore in the six quarter game, you couldn't tell it was that long by looking at the play on the field. Sure we were tired, but we kept pursuing and working. If you make up your mind, you can go all out every play of every game. Do that and you'll be playing a lot of football.

Defensive End
Barney Chavous
Denver Broncos

One reason Denver's Orange Crush defense is so effective is defensive end Barney Chavous. He doesn't receive the publicity of his counterpart, Lyle Alzado, but in six seasons Barney has started nearly every game. He is considered an excellent defender against the rush and backs have learned that, if he touches them, they're as good as down. Over two consecutive seasons Barney led the team by not missing a single tackle.

Barney is also an effective pass rusher in Denver's 3-4 defense. In 1976 he led the Broncos with 8 and ⅓ sacks. Chavous stands 6′3″ tall and weighs 252 pounds. In 1973 he was a second round draft choice of the Broncos after completing an outstanding college career at South Carolina State.

145

You might not guess it when you watch us on television, but defensive end is basically a finesse position, at least compared to our counterparts on the line, the defensive tackles. We have to be able to move quick and react. The need is to get around the offensive blockers quickly to reach the quarterback.

Don't get me wrong though. It's certainly important that you be able to hit and we do plenty of that. But many people think a defensive end has to be 6′ 8″ and 290 pounds to be effective. I've seen some guys weighing 175 and 185 pounds hit harder than guys 100 pounds heavier. A lot of it has to do with what's inside you.

I think there are four qualities that you should have to be a good defensive end. First, you need to enjoy football —to have the attitude that football is a fun game to play. Second, you need to be aggressive. Third, you need to be smart, and fourth, you must keep your poise. I'll talk more about the poise later, because I feel it is most important.

Notice I didn't say anything about being big. If you are big, that's a bonus. But don't try and let your size compensate for a lack in these other areas as I think they will have more influence on your chances for success than weight.

Defense seems to have changed its philosophy in recent years. It used to be that the offense would think of ways to attack and beat a certain defense, and the defense would react and try to stop each play. But on the Broncos and many other teams now, the defense, besides reacting, is trying to force things. One good thing about our 3-4 defense is that we can do so many things to confuse the offense.

There are a lot of things I can do out of each stance and formation that makes it hard for the offense to predict my movement. For example, they may run a sweep but if I'm charging hard outside on that play, they'll lose yardage. This is one reason I feel it's exciting to play defensive end—you can make things happen. You have to react, true, but you can also cause the offensive team a lot of headaches.

With that in mind, I'll give you some basics that I use for playing defensive end. Keep in mind that you can do a lot more as you learn to play. You may even come up with some moves no one else has thought up.

At defensive end, leverage is very important. That means you need to keep low, which starts with a good stance. Your stance needs to be comfortable and flexible so that you can move quickly in any direction.

I use three different stances: one for passing situations, one for running situations, and a third in goal line and short yardage situations. I'll describe each one.

In running situations, and you can tell these by the team's tendencies, I line up with my feet parallel to each other and perpendicular to the line of scrimmage. The rest of the stance is identical to that Mike McCoy described for defensive tackle.

For an obvious passing situation I line up in a sprinter's stance. All my weight is forward, my feet are back with one foot slightly ahead of the other—whichever way is comfortable for you. Use a three point stance so you have a free arm to use against the blocker.

For a goal line stand I use a four point stance. In this position all my weight is forward so I can move ahead with everything I've got. On a goal line play a defensive lineman doesn't need to read the play. His job is to protect his hole.

Back to the run. My first objective on the run is to defeat my blocker. Once you defeat and get rid of him, you can move toward the ball carrier. This is crucial because your first job is to protect your hole. With Denver, my area is the six hole between the tight end and tackle, or the five hole if the tight end is on the other side. Sometimes I have to protect the four and six hole. To cover these, I must defeat my blocker.

When I say defeat your blocker, I mean physically. Some guys try to go around their block, but you'll get in trouble doing that. You may make one or two great plays, but a good offense will notice you do that and burn you through the hole you should be plugging. So you should use your hands and physically keep the blocker off of you, then read the play and pursue.

Once you've defeated your blocker and read the play, you go for the ball carrier. Everyone covers his assigned area first, then worries about helping out. If you try to help out without first covering your hole, you aren't helping the team.

The defensive end's finesse comes in on pass plays. There are a few really big, strong players that can consistently overpower an opponent, but that's extremely rare nowadays, especially in the pros. So it's necessary to learn the right moves.

The defensive end has more distance to cover to the quarterback than does the defensive tackle, so he doesn't want to get tied up too long with the blocker. So I won't lose any time before the snap, I decide what move I want to put on the offensive tackle. It could be an inside move, an outside move, a power move, a speed move, or a combination of two of these.

After I've anticipated my move, I try to read the blocker to make sure my move will work. If he's set up to cover my move, I may have to compensate, or I may want to make the move to set up another one later on in the game.

For example, it's rather hard to rush inside because most offensive tackles try to protect the inside rush and allow you to go outside. I may then rush outside consistently. If I beat him once or twice with an outside move, he may start to compensate, and then I'll have a chance to take advantage of that and fake going outside and blow inside.

There are so many variations that it's hard to give you much, except to encourage you to use your creativity. Use your hands. Give him a blow to the helmet (if that's not illegal in your league). Use the swim technique that Mike explained.

Here's one other move you can use that is effective—the butt and jerk. You butt your man with your helmet and pull him toward you as he plants his feet. As you pull him toward you, you should be able to slip around him.

Another move you can make is the hit and spin. This way, as he's making contact, he's really not getting much of you because you're spinning by him, much as a running back spins off a tackler. I have other moves that don't even have names, and you'll develop your own as you go along.

Keep in mind that on a pass rush you don't necessarily have to tackle the quarterback in order to do your job. It's very difficult to get to him often. I led the Broncos in sacks with eight in 1976, so that meant I dumped the quarterback about once every other game.

But you can still disrupt the quarterback without sacking him. You can stick a hand in his face as he throws. Occasionally you can even knock down a pass if you get your arms up in the right place. Sometimes you can give him a good lick just as he releases the ball. That can psychologically be to your advantage because he may be gun shy about your coming the next time. All of these things can disrupt a quarterback and lower the effectiveness of his passing.

I haven't mentioned some of the other possibilities, such as the option play that is increasingly popular in high school and college. It's not used that much in the pros because of the risk of injury to the quarterback, but in college I faced it a lot. The aim of the option is to cause the defensive end to commit to either covering the quarterback or the running back who could take a pitch.

The problem is that you can't effectively cover both. You'll get burned most of the time. In college we assigned one defender to tackle the fullback, one to tackle the quarterback, and a linebacker to tackle the pitch back. No matter what those three men did, they got hit on every play. That is a very effective way to beat the option.

Other plays that will be run at you are the play action pass and the screen. On play action you have to play the run first and defeat your blocker. If you can read quick enough, you can get the blocker off balance and beat him on the pass rush. If the play is a screen, you still rush the quarterback. It's the linebacker's job to read the screen.

The only time you don't go after the quarterback is if you read from your keys that the play is definitely a screen.

These are basics, and they aren't intended to be complete by any means. It is very important that you keep in mind the four principles I mentioned at the beginning of this chapter, especially keeping your poise.

Football is a violent game, and when you have a lot of physical contact tempers will flare occasionally. For example, it's frustrating to beat your blocker and have a clear shot at the quarterback, only to have the tackle reach out and hold you. It makes you want to take that guy's head off.

Sometimes you're going to get beat by a good block, or you're going to miss a tackle. Does that mean you're going to get all upset and disappointed? If you do, you're liable to make another mistake on the very next play. *You can't play effectively when you're angry.*

In order to have poise you have to have confidence in yourself and your ability. You have to believe you can do the job. If you get beat you have to regroup and believe you can win the next round. Most people lose their poise because they've been beat and get confused. They forget what their assignment is, and they stop doing their best.

The thing that helps me the most in maintaining my poise is my Christian faith. I realize God has given me the ability to play football, and that gives me confidence. I realize that if I play my best, then I can relax knowing that the best team will win.

I don't always maintain my poise. Sometimes I make a mistake and get upset. There are times I've taken a swing at my opponent. Being a Christian doesn't mean you'll never make a mistake, but as a Christian, you have the means to regroup, to regain your poise.

I do it on the sidelines. I ask God to forgive me, which He promises to do because of Christ's death on the cross. Then I ask Christ to give me His strength to maintain my poise, and He does, because He promised in the Bible He would.

In 1977 there was quite a bit of publicity about the Christian faith on the Denver Broncos, particularly with our quarterback, Craig Morton. A lot of people didn't understand it, but I know it was responsible for the unity on our team. Not everyone on the team is a Christian, but we respect each other, and I believe the unity we have in Christ among the Christian players can't help but have a positive effect on the whole team.

Don't forget, football is a team game. You need to work together, but if you work together on your own without Christ, you end up hating each other. The only way you can have real unity is through Christ. It made a big difference on our team in helping us go to the Super Bowl.

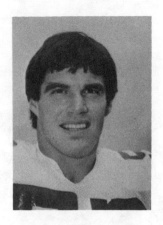

Linebacker
Bob Breunig
Dallas Cowboys

In Bob Breunig's third season with the Dallas Cowboys, he was asked to fill some very big shoes—those of middle linebacker Lee Roy Jordan who starred for fourteen years in the NFL. All Breunig did in 1977 was help the "Doomsday II" defense lead the team to the Super Bowl Championship.

Prior to the '77 season, Bob started at the strong side linebacker position, replacing another NFL veteran, Dave Edwards. In 1976 he had 63 tackles and 33 assists and led the team with three fumble recoveries. In 1977 he led Dallas in total tackles with 130, including 73 primary takedowns. In the Super Bowl versus Denver he made six tackles and tipped a pass that was intercepted by Aaron Kyle.

Bob's linebacker coach Jerry Tubbs states, "Bob is without question the most intense, hardest-working, serious football player I have ever seen. Bob's totally committed to performing even the practice drills as hard as he can. People can be intense about a lot of things, but Bob's type of intensity means to me he wants to do the job better than anyone else."

The outstanding linebackers in the National Football League are all-around ball players. You might call them the jack-of-all-trades for the defense. A linebacker has to be able to play the run and cover the pass equally well. Not only does he need to know how to tackle, but how to read plays and cover speedy running backs.

A linebacker needs to be quick and strong. He needs to be a complete athlete. He needs to be strong to take on linemen who are sometimes forty pounds heavier than he is. He needs to be able to move laterally, and he needs to adjust instantly to a run or pass. He doesn't need to be as fast as a running back or wide receiver, but he needs comparable quickness.

I was the middle linebacker for Dallas when we won the Super Bowl. That meant I had the responsibility of calling plays and making changes at the line, if necessary, before the snap. But even if you're an outside linebacker, you need to be a leader. By that I mean you need to be willing to study your defense and the other team's offense. You should know what your teammates are doing as well as they do. This will greatly enhance your effectiveness.

Now that I've said all of that, I hope I haven't discouraged you from playing this position. It is one of the most challenging and enjoyable in football, because you're involved in every play. But it's very difficult to teach you everything that would be useful to you in one short chapter. chapter.

The most important things I can tell you are to play with intense discipline and desire. Football is a contact sport and, of all the positions, you undoubtedly end up doing the most hitting as a linebacker. You have to want to hit people, but that's not enough. You must be a student. There is so much to learn about being a good linebacker, and you have to be willing to study both your job and the teams you will be facing. As you do this, your physical ability will be maximized so you can react and cover plays instantly.

Every defense is different, so it's hard to tell you much in the way of specifics. One of the most important things you need to learn is how to read keys. They are the life of a linebacker. You need to know what the play is going to be and where it will be run. If you can't read that within the first split second of a play, you'll be open to fakes and you'll lose that precious extra step that can make a difference between no gain and a first down.

For a middle linebacker the primary keys are the two guards and the center. The activity of these three men will usually dictate where the ball will go. If they drive block, I can usually assume the ball will be fairly close to me. My job is then to defeat my blocker and make the tackle.

If the guards are pulling then chances are there will be a sweep. If they drop back into pass protection block, it's obviously a pass. Beyond that you learn the tendencies of each blocker and begin to find little things they do that can alert you to a specific play. Perhaps on pass protection a guard's weight is back on his feet more than on a running play.

I don't rely exclusively on the guards and center for my keys. I sometimes key on one or both of the backs and what they do on the start of a play will tell me what the play is. I learn this by studying lots of film of the other team, but even if you don't watch film you can often pick up tendencies in the first series or two a team runs against you. And if you can watch a team play before you play them, that always helps. Another key, especially for an outside linebacker, is the tight end. He usually will block on running plays and run pass patterns on pass plays.

A linebacker, especially the middle linebacker, should be in on a lot of tackles. The linebackers should lead the team in tackles over the course of a season. To do that, you must be proficient in defeating your blockers so you can be free to make tackles.

The two methods I use to accomplish this are the forearm shiver and the two-handed palm shiver. I physically meet the blocker and try to defeat him. The forearm shiver should connect on a player's upper body and sometimes even on the helmet. But don't aim for his helmet every time because you can miss. The two-handed palm shiver is like a double straight arm—your palms meet your opponent on his shoulder pads. Both ways should stop the charge of the blocker and then allow you to move him out of your way to get to the ball carrier.

As far as covering a pass, the best keys are the guards and center. If they go into pass protection, you need to prepare to cover according to your assignment. If you are playing a zone, you will drop back into your area and react to what the quarterback does.

If you're playing man to man, usually your job is to cover a back. If he stays in the backfield to block, you should wait and cover the potential screen. If he comes out of the backfield, you will most always be at a disadvantage covering him, and you should understand that so you don't try to do more than you are physically capable of doing.

Most running backs will be faster than you. You can overcome that disadvantage by making contact with him— use a shiver or a bump to slow him down and disrupt his timing (the NFL now has a 5-yard rule; be sure to check the rules for your level). Also remember that you have backup help and that's why it is good to know what your teammates are doing behind you. Usually your responsibility is to cover him up to about fifteen to twenty yards from the line of scrimmage.

Covering man to man requires a lot of concentration. Nothing must distract you. I concentrate on my man's waist or belt buckle, never on his feet, shoulders, or head. Wherever his waist goes, that's where he'll go.

Your first job is to make the tackle. Beyond that, you would like to cause a fumble anytime you can. Your job is to stop the other team so your team can have the ball. A fumble does that quickly. However, you should never sacrifice making the tackle to try and force a fumble. The same principle is true with an interception.

Second, you must work at maintaining the inside position. By that I mean, you should cover his inside more. You don't want him to catch anything toward the center of the field. You will take away the curl or hook and give him a little slack on the outside.

The reason a linebacker prefers covering a sideline or out pattern is that the angles involved make it harder to complete the pass. Also, if they do run this pattern, he has a better angle from which to come in and make the tackle, knock the pass down, or possibly make an interception.

Third, you must hustle, hustle, pursue, pursue, work and keep on working. Hustle and pursuit are crucial for a linebacker because he should be involved in nearly every play. A linebacker should feel personally responsible for every play. After you first fulfill your assignment, you should always be willing to go where the football is and help make the tackle.

Probably the number one mistake young players make as linebacker is not pursuing at the proper angle. If you play racquetball, you know that a big part of that game is anticipating where the ball will go and heading there to intercept it. That's what you need to do with a ball carrier. You need to anticipate, based on his speed and direction, the point at which he can be cut off.

Linebackers should work hard to be in condition. There are a variety of areas you should work on. I feel these five should be part of every linebacker's off-season training program:

1. You need a long distance jogging program.
2. You need a good sprinting program to develop speed. Sprints should be run full speed covering any distance from ten to one hundred yards.
3. You need a weight lifting program that includes both quick, fast repetition with lighter weights as well as heavy, low repetitions. You want to build both strength as well as some bulk.
4. Flexibility and stretching exercises are very important for preventing injuries.
5. Finally, you want exercises that help in body control. The best for this are such sports as racquetball, handball, tennis, basketball or wrestling. These are all good auxiliary sports for football.

The most important thing I can tell you if you want to be a linebacker is to work hard. There is no substitute. You should study the position. Watch games on TV and try to learn from what linebackers are doing. I believe in studying films. Study your opponents and observe their tendencies.

You also have to be aggressive. Football is a contact sport, but you don't have to hurt people to play it hard. You should always play by the rules, but play as hard as you can.

I believe that God has given me a healthy body and the skills to be a good linebacker. Since God has given me this ability, it is my responsibility to do everything conceivable to fulfill my potential and become the best player I possibly can.

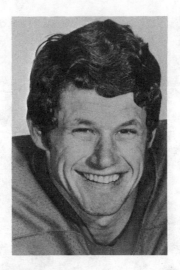

Defensive Back
Ray Easterling
Atlanta Falcons

Ray Easterling is proof that no odds are too great for someone who wants to play pro football. He was rejected by all his high school athletic teams as being too small until his father transferred him to a private school his junior year. Ray went to the University of Richmond and made the football team as a walk on and later won a scholarship.

The Atlanta Falcons drafted Ray in the ninth round but again his size—he's now listed as 6' tall and 192 pounds—made many observers feel he was too small and too slow to play. But he made the Falcons team and has survived six seasons, three as the team's starting free safety.

Ray is regarded as a player who tackles with reckless abandon. He's also picked up his share of interceptions—ten in three seasons beginning in 1975. He is part of a defense that in 1977 set an NFL record by allowing the fewest points over a 14-game season. Atlanta head coach Leeman Bennett says about Easterling: "He is smart, has good football savy, and always knows where the ball is."

In writing this chapter, I find it rather difficult to be very specific because a defensive back is more a reactor than anything else. He doesn't have set plays like the offensive team does. Sometimes I go out on the football field and feel disjointed because I don't know what is going to happen.

However, I've had enough experience in these pressure situations that I've learned how to react. It's hard to describe the pressure, playing as a cornerback or safety in pro football. I feel it takes a special breed of cat. You're the last line of defense. If you fail the other team has a touchdown. You can be successful against your man for 59 minutes, but if he beats you once for a touchdown and you lose the game, the fans are going to get on you.

I've seen a number of defensive backs come to camp and look super while practicing in shorts. You couldn't beat them. But put them in pads and they folded under the pressure of a game. It's not unusual to feel the pressure—every defensive back does, but you have to learn to cope with it and overcome it. You'll never succeed otherwise.

There is a big difference between playing cornerback and safety in the pros. The cornerback is usually one of the fastest players on the team and one of the best athletes. His responsibility is to cover a wide receiver man to man. His first responsibility is always the pass.

The safety is involved in more plays. I'd say the big difference between the safety and cornerback is the safety has to do more reading. He needs to read his keys and learn if the play is a run or a pass. He can key on the tight end or the guards, and what they do dictates his responsibility. He plays the pass first but has an important responsibility against the run.

Defensive back is a game of angles and a game of position. Since the safety plays inside and the cornerbacks outside, they have completely different angles. The only way you can cover the fast receivers today is to play the angles and to keep enough cushion between you and them. If you try to run with them, you'll get beat.

In the NFL we play a lot of zone defense, but even a zone eventually winds up with a man-to-man confrontation. When the man comes into your zone, you have to be able to play him man to man. The safety has a little more cushion to play with, however, than the cornerback.

First let me discuss the cornerback's job. The first thing he needs to do on the snap is establish position. Some like to line up inside the receiver, others outside the receiver. The idea is that you want to take something away from him. The receiver wants to come straight at you so you don't know which way he's going to break. He can go either way.

If you deny him a particular path you can establish the upper hand. For example, you may decide to take away his inside route. If he tries to go inside, you cut him off. If he keeps trying to go inside, you refuse to let him. But as you're doing this, you need to be ready to break quick to the outside if he does.

Your body position is important in coverage. You need to keep low and you do this by bending your knees and keeping your hips low. Your weight should be on the balls of your feet when you back peddle. Your feet should be about shoulder width. In this position you can move with the receiver. If you're back on your heels, you'll lose a step on the break and that's all the advantage a good receiver needs to beat you.

The idea on coverage is to break with your man, but in such a way that if he decides to cut back, he has to run through you. For example, let's say again you're taking away the inside. As he cuts, you now have such an angle that, if he decides to cut back inside, he'll run right into you. You're also in position to knock down the pass or to go deep with the receiver.

A crucial part of playing this position is to study your opponents. You need to know the tendencies of the quarterback and his receivers. What is their bread and butter play? What do they do well? Is your man fast? If so you need to play off of him a little more. Does he cut well? Then you want to cover him close. If he both runs fast and cuts well, then you have a problem; he's very tough to cover.

You can learn these tendencies by studying the team before you play them. It's harder to pick up the little things a receiver does on film than when you're playing directly on him. So it is very important that on the first couple of routes he runs in a game, you beat him bad. This is a very psychological game, and you need to get the upper hand immediately and set the tempo for the game.

For example, suppose he beats you on the post pattern right off the bat. Then next time you're looking to cover the post so you don't get beat again and he beats you to the corner. He's now got command of you for the game. So you need to beat him in his first pattern and establish your position. You need to establish some doubt in his mind about whether he should run that first pattern again.

Keep in mind at cornerback that your first job is to be in position to make the tackle. Second priority is to try to knock the pass down. Third, you'd like to make the interception. That's the best, but you can never sacrifice your position for the first two to make the interception unless it's a sure thing. I've seen too many young players get beat going for the interception and end up yielding six points.

Most interceptions come on mistakes. Either the ball is thrown poorly, or the pass pattern is run incorrectly. If the receiver runs a good route and the quarterback throws a good pass, you probably can't intercept it. The only way you can intercept in that situation is to anticipate the route and beat the receiver to it. You have to be careful here though. You may assume he's running a curl and run up for the interception, and suddenly he's run a curl and go and you're beaten. So don't overplay your man.

The cornerback position is not quite as complicated as safety. Safety is a completely different position. You have to be concerned with the run as well as the pass. The safety assignment can take two forms. The strong safety usually plays closer to the line of scrimmage opposite the tight end. It's a difficult position because he has to react quickly.

Many teams run at him, and he has to turn in the sweep and prevent the long gain.

I play a free safety, which means I'm the last man back. In the NFL, the free safety still plays the run. You need to be able to read the play and react, to go to the ball without thinking about it. That's why rookies have a hard time in the NFL at first. They may have a lot of ability; they may be fast and quick, but they don't read and react quickly. So experience is very important at this position.

Once you've read the play as a run, there's no sense in staying back and waiting. You don't want the runner to get into the open field where he can maneuver and cut. I like to come up and cut down his running room. The more people around him, the harder it is for him to break loose. The basic tackling technique is exactly what Jeff Siemon says in his chapter. Keep in mind that many times a defensive back is one on one with the receiver or back in the open field. So it is very important that you wrap your arms completely around him.

As far as covering the receiver, that will depend on your assignment. Some teams allow the free safety to be just that—free to go where the ball is. Others want him to cover a specific man; that will depend on your coach. There are three important principles that will help you cover a receiver.

First, don't watch his feet, head or shoulders. Watch his belt buckle, his stomach or his chest. They will move with him and he can't fake you with them. A lot of young players try to watch the receiver's head, but you'll surely get faked out that way because he can move his head one way and go the other.

Second, intimidation is very important in covering a receiver. When he catches the ball, you need to unload on him. You need to hit him as hard as you can. If you do that (hitting him fair, never dirty) he'll be thinking of you the next time. A lot of balls are dropped because of that. In the pros we don't get a lot of opportunities to hit a receiver hard. So I try to take advantage of every opportunity I get.

Third, position is crucial. One thing that is helpful is to use the sideline. There's no sense covering your man very close if he's near the sideline. You can close in quickly if he catches the ball and knock him out of bounds. But if you stay back at an angle until then, he has very little chance of cutting back inside and going around you for the long gain.

In 1977 the Atlanta Falcons set an NFL record by allowing the fewest points in a season. I feel the reason we did was that we hit, we hustled and we pursued. We swarmed the ball carrier. If someone missed a tackle there was always another covering. We had eleven guys going to the football all the time. If the play went to one sideline, eleven guys converged there. We wanted to have four or five guys hit the ball carrier before he hit the ground. It was very effective and discouraged a lot of teams. That's the key to a successful defense—pursuit, never quitting until the play is over.

It is very important that you develop your skills as a football player. If you're going to be a defensive back, do what I did. I found out what my strengths and weaknesses were. I worked on my weaknesses. There is a tendency among athletes to work on what is easiest for them to do, but that won't make you a better athlete.

For example, I've always been pretty quick, but I've never had that flat out speed. So every off season, I go out on the track and work on my speed. I don't worry about my quickness—I'll keep that.

Perhaps you have speed but have trouble with your lateral quickness. Then you'd better work on that. Perhaps you're quick and have speed, but you have trouble catching a football. Then work on that. Work with your coach and have him give you an idea of what you should work on during the off season. The off season is the time for you to work on your weaknesses.

For a defensive back, one skill you need that no other position requires, at least not to the same degree, is running backwards. There's no set way to do this. Some guys are more comfortable staying low; others like to run more straight up. That depends on the individual. But whatever way you run, you must be able to cut quickly.

That takes a lot of practice. You should practice covering people. Have a friend run pass patterns in your backyard. Practice back peddling on him and cutting to cover him. That's the only way it will become natural to you.

Don't ever get to the point where you think you have it all as a football player. No one does. You need a combination of skills and qualities, and that's what makes football a great game. Some guys are fast, but they're not agile. Others are agile and fast, but they don't think ahead. Some guys are fast, agile, and think well, but they make a lot of mistakes. Some may not have determination. There is always something you can be working on.

As I've mentioned, it's not just your physical skills. Who you are as a person will have a lot to do with how well you succeed. I made it as a football player because I was determined that my size wasn't going to beat me, no matter what anyone else thought.

But remember, football will not always be with you. What happens to you when you don't have football? I believe Christianity has the answer to that question. For me, the joy of knowing Jesus Christ more than exceeds any pleasure I get from playing football.

Special Teams
Brad Cousino
Toronto Argonauts

He may not be very big by pro football standards. He's only 5′ 11¾″ tall and weighs 212 pounds. He's much too small to be a defensive lineman—he was a middle guard in college—and even for a linebacker, the pros like their men a little bigger. But don't tell Brad Cousino that he can't play pro football.

Brad has played five years as a specialist. He's the man who makes special teams go. More and more teams are recruiting players like Brad solely to go down and bust wedges, cover punts, block on kickoffs, and the like.

Cousino was not drafted by the pros despite the fact he made every all-American team his senior year. He signed as a free agent with the Cincinnati Bengals and played his first season on their special teams. He then had stops with the Chicago Bears and New York Giants before joining the Pittsburgh Steelers late in the 1977 season. In 1978 he played for Toronto of the Canadian Football League.

I want to make this point right away. If you're playing on special teams, you are a very important part of your team. In no way are you a second stringer. You can make or break your team. You can do a tremendous amount to help your team win. If you are a starter and also play on special teams, you must play as intensely as you do during regular downs. What happens on special teams will often decide a game.

In pro football the teams who make the playoffs win four or five games because of their special teams. In 1975 Dallas could credit six victories directly to the play of their special teams. That's significant. If you will take seriously what I tell you in this chapter, your team whatever level you're playing on, could win two to four extra games this next season!

I didn't always feel this way about special teams. In college the guys who didn't start and played on special teams acted like they were second rate—and they played like it. But when I got to the pros, I saw an entirely different emphasis and realized the importance of this phase of football.

Attitude is crucial on special teams. If you think you aren't important to the team, then you'll play that way, and you may well cost your team a game because of it. You must change that attitude. If it weren't for special teams, I wouldn't have played pro football. I'm too small according to the thinking of most coaches. There was a place for me, however, and there's a place for you if you have the right perspective.

There are three attitudes that you must have on special teams. First, you have to believe you're the best player on that field and that no one can knock you down. Second, you have to decide that whoever has the ball, you are going to tackle him. *You have to get him.* Third, nothing will stop you. If you get knocked down, you get back up *immediately* and keep going. Nothing will keep you from making the tackle. You must never think that someone else will do it; you must want to make every tackle.

The game of football has become so scientific today that it's very difficult to turn the game around quickly, but special teams can do that. They can make the fifty yard turnaround and change the momentum. The hitting on special teams is much more intense. The play is faster and more wide open. You have to want to hit, and you must not mind being hit. The special teams create excitement.

Perhaps the number one special team in my mind is the kickoff unit, especially at the start of the game. This team can set the tempo for the whole game. If the kickoff team can pin the other team deep in their territory, they've gained a great upper hand. But if the other team gets a return to their forty or forty-five, usually they will score at least three points on that drive; they then have the upper hand.

When I line up for the kickoff, I like to lay back about eight yards and get a good running start. I need it because I'm not very fast. I run only about 4.8 or 4.85 in the 40. Despite that, I'm usually one of the first players to get to the return man. A running start helps.

As I line up the first thing I do is look at the front line to see who will block me. From then on I keep my eyes on the ball carrier. It is important to know who will block you so you can avoid the block if at all possible. Each player has a lane he is responsible for. That's an area about five yards wide extending down to the goal line. You must stay in your lane, and you must stay on your feet. Kick return men are so quick today that one good block and they can break loose.

But if you do get knocked down, you must bounce back up. It's easy to get knocked down because you're moving so fast. But never, never, never stay down. A block should hardly slow you down because you bounce back up immediately.

As you get close to the ball carrier, you'll be coming toward the wedge, the wall of usually four blockers who lead the way for the return. Usually they block two on one and try to knock down two men. My job is usually that of wedge buster. Most people think that means I drive through these men. But that's not the case. The only time

172

I try to go through the wedge is if the ball carrier is only a yard or so behind them. Then I figure if I can pile into the wedge I can throw the blockers back into the runner and thus destroy the return.

But usually the return man is between five and seven yards behind the wedge so he can follow their blocks. So I don't want to sacrifice myself. I want to make the tackle. So I usually use a handshiver. I hit one or two blockers with the palms of my hands keeping my arms extended. This keeps them off me and allows me to bounce off easily to go after the tackle.

I like to get a good shot at the return man. I'm disappointed if I don't get at least two or three tackles on kickoffs each game. If I can tackle a man inside the 20, that can set the tempo for the entire game. It's a tremendous psychological boost for me and my team.

After kickoff coverage the next most important special team in my mind is punt coverage. Again, you don't want to be knocked down. First, you have to block to keep the other team off the punter, then you have to cover and form a net. Your job is to flush the return man out.

You do this by reading which way the return is set up. The other team will have a return to the right, left, or up the middle, and all the blockers will set up accordingly. However, the coverage team again fills the lanes. You want a couple of your men, usually the ends, to flush out the return man from behind his protection and run him into your other tacklers.

The ends are so important on this because they are allowed to leave on the snap. If the punt is high they can get down and cover the man and run him into the rest of the team which is pursuing. I must emphasize the need to stay on your feet. On a punt return the other team can get some super blocks on you if you are not alert. I'll tell you how later. If you get knocked down, you must get back up immediately. It doesn't take much to spring a good return man. Billy "White Shoes" Johnson of Houston is so effective because he can take on one block and be gone.

You have to want to get that ball carrier, but you can't run down the field like a madman. While you want to get down the field fast, if you go too fast, you won't be able to cut and make the tackle—so maintain control.

Next in importance is the punt return team. This team can also change the tempo of a game. A good return of fifteen or twenty yards changes a lot of things for your offense. They have greater flexibility for play selection. In pro ball, field position is what wins games. It means everything.

What is even more devastating is blocking a punt. It means an automatic fifty or sixty yard turnaround. When I was playing with the New York Giants, we were tied late in the first half against Detroit. With about two or three minutes left to play, I broke through and blocked a Lion punt and we recovered on the four. We quickly scored, went into the locker room with momentum and ended up winning the game. That play turned the game completely around in our favor.

There is a technique to blocking kicks. In college I blocked between fifteen and twenty punts and field goals. It's a little tougher in the pros. The key is to be quick off the snap. You need a perfect takeoff. I do that by keying on the center. Right before the snap, he'll flex his hand, or thumbs, and in some way move when he's starting his snap. You take off at that instant.

My attitude on this is that I have to get to the ball. That's why the initial jump is key because you don't want to be blocked. Usually when you get past the line, you have to beat the safety valve (usually a fullback) to get to the punter. I usually do this with some sort of fake. Then you want to aim about four or five yards in front of where the kicker lines up. If you come in from the side, you'll want to lunge in front of the punter to intercept the ball just after it leaves his foot. If you come up the middle, you jump straight up as high as you can. Don't be afraid of the ball. It may hurt for a moment, but if you block it, you'll be so excited, you'll hardly notice any pain.

Never risk hitting the punter in order to get the ball. You must be sure you can touch the ball. A roughing the

174

kicker penalty is inexcusable. It kills you. Always go for the ball, not the kicker. About the only time you can even come close to justifying it is late in a game if you're behind and there's no other hope. Otherwise, stay away from the punter!

As far as blocking for the return, I always take a good crack at the guy on the line first. I always make him think I'm going for the kicker. That way, he never knows when I'm really going in. Then we go into our wall. Say we're returning right. We'll run down the line of scrimmage to the field numbers, then run down field to meet the return man.

You can get some super blocks now, because you're coming at the other team from the blind side. They will have to turn to get the runner, and as they turn, you can lower the boom. Here again, it is a psychological game. You're both going full speed and if you connect well, he'll be looking out for you next time instead of the ball carrier. That gives your runner an advantage.

Two things to keep in mind here. First, stay on your feet. Hit the man about his waist or higher. That way you are still on your feet to get another block on someone else. The only time I try a cross body block is if I feel I can take two men out at the same time.

The other thing concerns clipping. Clipping is a dumb mistake. Two things will keep you from being called for clipping. First, never hit a man if you see any part of the back of his jersey. Second, always make sure your head is in front of your man. You shouldn't get called if you do this.

Regarding kickoff returns. Your goal here is to get the ball past your 35. That gives your offense good field position. But you can't do that unless you knock someone down. It's hard to block high on the numbers, so I try to cross body block. But don't block so low that he can hurdle you. I try to catch him about waist high. You have to realize that the other team doesn't want to hit you in this play. Your job is to put a good shot on the man you are assigned to; knock him down, tie him up—make him concentrate on you rather than the ball carrier.

Let's turn to the field goal teams. When you're blocking for a field goal, you want to block low. And you must give absolutely no ground. The technique is not a drive block. You basically want to block with your shoulder to the inside gap. The guys on the end basically have to block two men. First, you pinch inside like the other blockers, but you bounce off that block and knock the cornerman off stride. That man has to have perfect timing to get to the ball, so even knocking him one step off is usually enough to do the job.

The key thing in blocking for the field goal is allowing no penetration. This is especially true on long field goal attempts where the trajectory is lower. If the defenders penetrate even a yard, they often can jump up and get a hand on the ball.

On the other side of the line, if you're trying to block a field goal attempt, you have about 1.6 seconds to do it. If the other team takes 1.7 or 1.8 seconds, they've taken too long. The key again is getting off quick on the snap. You want to make yourself as small as possible because there's little room for you to get through. You need to twist your shoulders until they're perpendicular to the line of scrimmage. Then you try to claw your way through anyway you can.

This is no time to be fancy. I want to block the ball any way possible. If I don't get very deep, I jump and try to reach the ball with my hand. You don't get the ball very often, but when you do it can be a big play. Even extra points are important. Many games have been decided because someone managed to block an extra point.

It is so important that you have pride in doing your job if you're on special teams. You can change the course of a ball game, but you have to want to do it. You have to realize you're very important out there. If you aren't a starter but you do the job on special teams, you may soon get a chance to start on the offensive or defensive unit.

Perhaps one experience I had in college proved to me that you should never, never quit. We were playing Kentucky my senior year at Miami of Ohio. We were undefeated and the media were playing up a confrontation I was to have with Rick Nuzum (now with the Packers) who was Kentucky's all-American center.

We had a terrific battle. It was an exciting game. I had blocked one kick for a field goal, and that was the difference in our being ahead 14-10. But the Kentucky quarterback was giving us fits with his option play. We had been unable to stop him all afternoon. With only a few minutes left to play, they ran another option play. Nuzum blocked me down and the quarterback took off. He was really fast and had caught our defensive backs out of position. But I didn't stay on the ground. I got up and started chasing him. It was obvious he was going to score, but I still kept running. Forty five yards later, I caught him and brought him down on the five yard line!

I still can't believe I made that play. We held them on that goal line stand and won the game. It goes to show that you must never quit. If you keep trying and refuse to stay down, you can make things happen. That is especially true on special teams.

In what other area of football does one have the opportunity to make the big play more often than when the ball is being kicked or punted? One great smashing tackle will squirt the ball loose; a timely block will allow a running back to score a TD; a blocked punt will completely turn a game in your favor; a fumble recovery will change the momentum. It all comes down to *you* and your desire and attitude. *You* can make all these things happen. *You* will make them happen when *you* believe in yourself and realize how important you are to your team.

Running Back Kicks
Mike Fuller
San Diego Chargers

Mike Fuller has done a yeoman job for the San Diego Chargers, despite being only 5′ 9½″ tall. His first two seasons he returned both punts and kickoffs. In 1977 he was due to concentrate only on his job as the team's strong safety, but an injury to Johnny Rodgers forced him back into the punt return job.

On his first punt return of 1977 against New Orleans, he returned the kick 88 yards for a touchdown. It was the second longest in club history. He ranked fourth in the NFL and in the AFC over the season with a 12.9 yard return average. In 1978, he returned 39 punts an average of 11.2 yards per kick, fifth best in the AFC. Entering the 1979 season, Fuller was third among active AFC returners with 136 punt returns for 1,642 yards and two touchdowns. His average is a consistent 12.1 yards per return.

Mike is San Diego's strong safety and also holds the ball on field goals and extra points. In 1976, he ran seven yards for a touchdown out of field goal formation to wrap up a 23-7 victory over Kansas City. In 1977, he led the Chargers in interceptions with five.

179

By far the most important attribute a return man must have is a combination of speed and quickness. If you don't have those, you shouldn't be running back kicks. Speed is probably a little more important on kickoffs, while quickness is crucial on punt returns.

The other thing you need is good hands. You need to be able to catch the ball on the run. You also need to be able to catch the ball consistently in difficult situations: with pressure, with wind, with the ball taking crazy bounces.

Catching the ball on punts and kickoffs is similar to what a centerfielder does when there's a runner on third base. He wants to come in and catch the ball running toward home so he has the momentum to throw the runner out. It's the same principle in returning kicks. The one thing you do not want to do is catch the ball while you're backing up. You lose precious time and steps if you have to stop and reverse gears to move forward. It can mean the difference between a little gain and a good return.

Let's cover the kickoff return first. If you're returning a kick, you need to have good speed for 70 to 80 yards, and you need to be able to follow your blocks. You will have a wedge or wall in front of you on about the 20 (this will vary according to how far the other kicker can boot the ball) and you will be lined up 10 to 15 yards behind that wall.

Before the kickoff, you decide on a play. You'll either go up the middle or toward one sideline (determined by the coach or called in the huddle) and the wall blocks accordingly. You need to be aware of where the wall is and where it is setting up.

First you must catch the ball. When you catch it you must be at least stationary, and it's better if you're leaning forward. I repeat, do not get caught going backwards when you catch the ball. It's better for you to go too far back and run up to catch the ball.

The technique for catching the ball is not at all like catching a pass. A kickoff is usually going end over end and you need to cradle it in your mid-section. That stops the momentum of the ball and keeps you from hurting

*Catching ball
on kickoffs and
putting it away*

your fingers. Use your chest or stomach as a backstop.

What you do not want to do is try to catch the ball to your side. You should position your arms and hands as if you were going to catch a flyball using Willie Mays' basket catch style. Your hands should be out about waist high and five or six inches apart. You want to make sure the ball is in front of your body so it won't get by you. You can actually catch the ball anywhere between your hands and your forearms.

Once you've got control of the ball, put it away immediately. If you're going on a sideline return, you should probably put it away on the side you're running to. Otherwise, use whatever arm is most comfortable.

A mistake many young players make is in judging the ball. It's easy to get out of position so you can't catch it with your body. You need to judge the wind before every return and adjust accordingly.

Another problem is catching the squibber. Most kick-offs will go end over end. The squibb kick is a ball the kicker boots short. When it bounces, especially on synthetic turf, the ball can do all kinds of tricky things and it's hard to catch. It's an excellent weapon for a kickoff team that wants to disrupt your timing.

On a squibber then, you want to do everything you can to catch the ball before it hits the ground. Since it will probably be a line drive, if you do catch it in the air, you can usually get a very good return. But if it bounces, you need to stay back. Stay low and keep your eyes on it like an infielder would a ground ball. Then look it into your hands. It is very important that you have control of the ball before you try to run with it.

Ideally, after the catch you're already moving forward and you've put the ball away. Usually the kick will be in the middle of the field. Even if you have a sideline return, you want to start up the middle before you make your cut. The key now is speed. You want to be about six or seven yards behind your wall as they start to make their blocks. As they make their blocks, you should be right on them in order to take advantage of those blocks.

The problem some runners have is that they are too slow getting up to the wedge and thus the blocks don't do any good. The defense has time to get back up and still make the tackle. But you don't want to be too close to the wedge before they've made their blocks, because then the defense can simply pile you up. This takes quite a bit of experience. You need to have the instinct of a back to take the most advantage of the blocks.

Once you're past the wedge, it's up to you to get all the yardage you can. But you can still help your blockers. For example, suppose a defender is coming down the right sideline. The blocker wants to block him toward the sideline. You should make a move toward the sideline to draw the defender that way, and then as the blocker makes his block, cut back inside.

Our objective on the Chargers is to return every kick to at least the 25 or 30. That's the minimum. Anything beyond that is good execution, and depends primarily on what the return man can get. Because everyone is so spread out, it's hard to get many extra blocks on a kickoff, compared to the punt return.

If the kickoff is toward one sideline rather than down the middle, you should simply take off up that sideline. Do not cut back across the field, even if you have a sideline return called for the other side. We have a code word on the Chargers that I yell if the kick is the wrong side, and it calls off the play and alerts the blockers to improvise as best they can.

Coaches hate to see someone run across the field on a kickoff. You want to move upfield. So if the kick is near the sideline, move up that sideline and make whatever yardage you can.

If you don't return a kickoff past your 20, usually one of three things happened. One is that the kick was extremely high. Ray Guy from Oakland kicks the ball so high that it hangs in the air for about 4.5 seconds. This allows the coverage to get down before the return team can make any blocks. The wedge usually doesn't start blocking until you've caught the ball.

The second possibility is that you've bobbled the ball, or there is indecision as to who should catch it. Since there is often more than one man who can return a kick, it is important before the kick to decide who will make the decision. Usually the primary returner will decide whether to take it, or call for a teammate to take it. If you don't take the return, you should get in front of the man who does and watch him. Get about five yards in front and watch him catch it. The reason for this is that if he bobbles the ball, you can help recover it. When he catches it, you throw a block at the first enemy jersey you meet.

The third possibility on a short return is a missed blocking assignment.

Now let's talk about punt returns. You need to practice catching punts even more than you do kickoffs, because the ball can do more things. The most common possibilities are: 1. The ball can spiral down. This is hard to catch as the ball comes down very hard. The kcy is to keep your hands and arms together so the ball won't bore through them. Use your chest or abdomen to back it up and cradle it. 2. The ball can float. This happens when it doesn't turn over. Usually you have to back up a little more to catch this as it will travel a little further. 3. If the ball goes off the side of the kicker's foot, the ball will curve from the sideline toward the center of the field. If it starts left, it will curve back right and vice versa. So you need to adjust for that.

You need a lot of concentration on a punt. You have to judge immediately what kind of a kick it is, and position yourself accordingly. Remember you want to be at least leaning forward, maybe even running forward as you make the catch. I've caught punts enough now to be able to peek downfield quickly before the catch, and still get my eye back on the ball. I don't recommend this for you. Your first job is to catch the ball. If you drop it, the other team can recover for a super long gain.

As soon as you catch the ball, you have to make some quick decisions. If the punt has good hang time (4 to 4.5 seconds is great), there will no doubt be a couple of defenders close to you. So immediately you need to decide how to avoid them. You need to put a couple of moves on to shake them, and this is where your quick feet are essential.

When do you fair catch? I recommend you do what our team does—have a safety man about ten yards in front of you. His number one job is to block the first man down the field. Second, he is in a position to tell you whether or not to fair catch. If I don't hear anything, I run it back. If I should fair catch it, he yells that to me. This takes the

pressure off me and allows me to just concentrate on the ball.

But if your coach doesn't put a safety in, then the best I can say is you need to develop the instinct to know when to fair catch. That takes practice. In my first three years in the NFL, I made only two fair catches.

If the other team is punting inside your 50, so there is a chance the ball could land inside the 10, line up on the 10. If you have to back up to catch the punt, let it go. If you can run up on it, take it. If you let it go, you can either block the first man who comes down, or you can move over to the side and signal for a fair catch in order to draw the other team away from the ball and allow it to go into the end zone.

On a runback, once you sidestep those first one or two defenders, you usually have a second to break for your wall. Your team will call a play before the punt that will tell you where to run the ball back. Unlike the kickoff you always move to get behind the wall with one exception. You never want to run backwards and risk losing a lot of yardage. Most teams will let you run laterally all you want.

From there you play your blocks and get as much as you can. It is important on both punts and kickoffs to keep your legs driving at all times. Your success depends on breaking tackles. You should be able to shake many of the arms and hands that grab you. You want to make more than one person tackle you. I've seen times when a defense will relax because they think you're going down, but you keep your legs driving, break free and the defense can't recover.

Once in a great while, everything comes together in the ultimate perfect play. That happened on my first punt return of 1977, after my teammate Johnny Rodgers was injured. The punter for New Orleans outkicked his coverage—by that I mean he kicked the ball so deep that his teammates couldn't get down to cover before I caught it.

I ran across the field after catching the ball and got behind the wall. It was the best blocking wall I've ever seen and it was relatively easy to follow their blocks and go 88 yards for a touchdown. In all of my years of running back kicks, including more than 10 for touchdowns (in college and pros) this was the first time I can remember not being touched on a return.

That's the ultimate; but it doesn't happen very often. Still, if you follow these guidelines, and if you have the speed and quickness, you can be successful on punts and kickoffs. If you average more than 10 yards per punt return, you're helping your team. And if you consistently return the kickoff past the 30, you're giving your offense good field position.

The key to success in running back kicks is confidence. You can't be afraid of dropping the ball out there. You need to practice hard so you are confident you can catch the ball any time under all conditions. It will come if you're willing to work at it.

Punting
Duane Carrell
St. Louis Cardinals

Have foot, will travel. That was the story of Duane
Carrell's career in pro football. A graduate of Florida
State (1971) where he was punter and place kicker, Duane
was unable to find a football job until 1974 when he signed
with the Jacksonville Sharks of the World Football League.
There he showed his ability by averaging 41.1 yards on
93 punts before the team folded. Dallas then picked him
up for the last half of the 1974 season.

After that he spent one year with the Los Angeles
Rams, another with the New York Jets, and finally wound
up with the St. Louis Cardinals before his voluntary retire-
ment in 1978. The longest punt of his career carried 72
yards for the New York Jets in 1976. That year he also set a
Jets team record with 81 punts, averaging 39.7 yards per
kick. During his career, Duane averaged better than 39
yards per punt and never had one blocked.

*Hand positions
for receiving
snap on punts*

There's a misconception that punting and field goal kicking is for the guy who can't do anything else. That's simply not true. A punter needs to be a good athlete. He's not just using a strong leg. He's using his whole body, so there's a lot of technique involved. A punter needs good eye-hand and eye-foot coordination.

When setting up for a punt, each person has a little different style. I like to lean forward slightly with my arms hanging down. Others like to stand straight up and extend their hands toward the center. That's a matter of personal preference.

Most punters in the NFL line up about 15 yards behind the line of scrimmage. How far you drop back depends on your playing level. For young players in Pop Warner and similar programs, probably eight or ten yards is sufficient. You should only drop as deep as your center can snap the ball to you.

Your first job is to catch the ball so you should feel very comfortable handling a football. You need to be able to react quickly because very few centers can give you a perfect snap everytime. The ball is liable to be anywhere on the snap so you need good hands. It wouldn't hurt you to practice with the receivers and get used to catching the football.

Most punters like the laces facing straight up when they punt. You rarely get a good kick when the laces are down. You may need to spin the ball so the laces are properly positioned. Mike Bragg is the only punter in the NFL that I know of who punts with the laces on the side, although others do when they're in a hurry.

I grip the ball with the point in the palm of my right hand and the fingers wrapping the end. The left hand is more of a guide. It holds the front of the ball, but the right hand does most of the work.

The level you hold the ball varies with each person. I like to hold it about chest high. Some like to hold it around their waist; others as high as their face. However, the higher you hold the ball, the more margin there is for error.

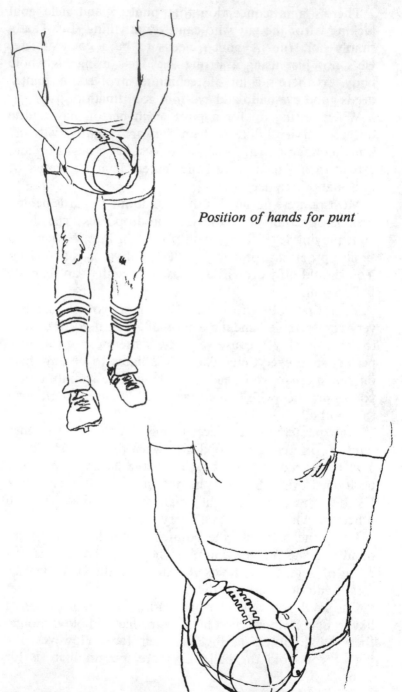

Position of hands for punt

It is important to keep the ball level, parallel with the ground. You can hold it at an angle—I have the nose of the ball slightly to the left of perpendicular to the line of scrimmage. This helps me get better contact, with less chance of hitting the ball off the side of my foot. But keep the ball level—in such a way that if you were to drop it, it would bounce straight back up.

As far as dropping the ball, think about placing the ball on your foot. All you want to do is drop the ball. Don't push it out or down. Don't do anything except let go. As you pull your hands away from the ball, it should drop flat and your foot should meet the ball about knee height.

There are various theories about the footwork of punting. Most coaches teach either a two-step or three-step approach. I believe most punters in the NFL use a three-step. Some coaches say that a two-step allows you to get the ball away quicker, but I haven't found that true. You can be just as quick on the three-step, and I can keep better balance.

To do the three-step, I take the snap with my left foot slightly forward of my right foot. Again, that's a matter of preference, but I feel quicker this way. When I get the snap, I take my first step with the left foot, then step with the right and my third step with the left foot is the longest. I kick off this step.

The key to successful punting is to get your whole body into the kick. The three-step approach gives you the momentum to do that. You want your body leaning forward as you begin your kick. When you finish, your shoulders should be straight up. The momentum of the kick should carry you forward. Your feet should leave the ground and land a foot or two forward of the spot where you kicked.

A lot of coaches say your knee should be in your face when you complete your punt. I think the important thing is to bring your foot up through the ball, and it should wind up wherever is comfortable for you. Most punters get their foot up about face level. I like to get mine even a little higher than that.

A lot of young players are good punters until it comes to facing defensive pressure. The only way to beat that is to keep under control. You have to take your steps quickly and kick. It takes a lot of practice. When I start training camp each summer, it takes me about two and a half seconds from the snap to the kick. But as I work each day it begins to go down and by the time the season starts it's down to about two seconds, which is pretty good.

You have to be confident you can do it any time. The temptation is to look at who's coming toward you and try and rush your kick. If you try to kick faster, you tend to swing your leg harder and that fouls up your timing. You're likely to shank the ball. You must keep under control and not try to kick any harder than usual. Concentrate on the ball, not on the other team. This comes through practice every single day.

Because of the nature of football today, especially in the NFL, hang time is very important. If a punter can keep the ball in the air between four and five seconds, his team will usually be able to prevent a return. If your kicks aren't high enough to satisfy your coach, try holding the ball a few inches higher on your drop and do everything else the same. Don't try to kick harder though. Keep a good easy motion.

The only time I don't worry much about height is when I'm kicking out of the end zone. Then it is more important to get good distance, rather than height, and simply take your chances on a return. If you kick away from the return man, you may get a good roll and put them further back.

Another thing that causes panic among punters is wind. When the wind is blowing in your face, the temptation is to try to kick the ball harder to compensate. I still make this mistake. The most important thing is to try and relax and simply try to give the ball a good spiral motion. That way it will bore through the wind. If you wobble the ball the wind will catch and slow it. Don't kick the ball quite as high in this situation either.

With the wind in your face, the ball probably won't go quite as far. You'll simply have to be satisfied with a little less. A lot of success when punting into wind simply depends on your mental attitude. When I punted for the Jets, we had wind everyday at our practice site. So when I kicked on Sunday in windy Shea Stadium, I was prepared.

Another thing coaches want their punters to do now is kick in the coffin corner. This is even more important now that missed field goals outside the 20 will be returned to the line of scrimmage. Now coaches often prefer a punt.

The key to punting in the coffin corner is being able to kick the ball straight consistently. Some kickers get great distance on their punts, but can't control their direction. That hinders their being able to kick in the corner.

The way I practice it is to take two helmets, or shoes, and put one on the goal line and the other on the 10, right on the sideline. I practice kicking to this target from various spots from the 35 on back.

The St. Louis Cardinals had a different philosophy on these types of kicks. Rather than have me aim for the sideline they preferred I simply try and kick the ball in that area. With a good coverage team I prefer this. I practice the same way, as far as setting up the markers, and work on getting an easy motion on my kick and laying the ball in this zone. I call it the soft shoe. It's the exact same form you use on every punt, but simply an easier kick. The only way to do it is to practice it.

There are four mistakes that inexperienced punters commonly make. First, many young players try to kick the ball too hard. I still make this mistake occasionally. You think that the harder you kick the ball, the farther it will go, but that's not true. Punting is a lot like a golf swing. Your technique causes the distance. A golfer who tries to swing too hard will lose his form and, more often than not, get less distance.

The second mistake is a poor drop. Young players tilt the ball or push it as they drop. You simply want to hold it level and let go. Practice developing a smooth drop. Drop it a few times without kicking. If it bounces straight back up, it's a good drop.

Third, develop a smooth, fluid motion. A lot of young kickers are "herky jerky." They stop or hesitate in the middle of their steps, and when they do that, they lose all of their momentum. Even a strong leg won't compensate for that. It is better to have a weak leg and good body momentum than to have a strong leg but no momentum.

Fourth, don't take your eyes off the ball. There is a temptation to look up to see where the ball is going before you kick it—don't. Work on keeping your eye on the ball until it leaves your foot.

Some people wonder if you need to use a special shoe. I suggest you use whichever football shoe feels the most comfortable. It takes me a while to get used to a shoe and break a pair in so I don't change in mid-season.

You need to be in good condition as a punter. You should work on your conditioning all year. I find jogging is very good. I try to run one to three miles several times a week. Also riding a bicycle is very good because it strengthens the muscles you use in kicking.

As far as weights, don't overdo it. I lift a little before the season to strengthen my quads, knees and hamstrings. But once the season starts, I stay away from the weights. I think it is more important to keep loose. I can't over emphasize the importance of stretching exercises every day before you punt. In addition, games like racquetball, handball and basketball are good for conditioning and for eye-hand coordination. Soccer is very helpful for youngsters in developing good kicking motion.

Place Kicking
John Smith
New England Patriots

The first American football game John Smith ever attended, he played in for the New England Patriots. He was a soccer player in England and as he visited the United States as a summer camp instructor, he was asked to try kicking a football. Based on that the Patriots invited him to a tryout.

He didn't make the team in 1973 but spent an apprentice season with the minor league New England Colonials where he set Atlantic Coast League records with 36 straight extra points and 19 for 21 field goals, including a 48 yarder.

The left footed kicker got another chance in 1974 and made the Patriots. He's been the New England kicker ever since and his record is outstanding. He missed only five extra points in his first four seasons, twice going 33-33 over a full 14 game schedule. He has also kicked field goals with amazing accuracy, nearly sixty-five percent over his career. His powerful left foot has given New England 315 points over four years.

I didn't really know what to expect when I came to the United States to try out for American football. But it seemed like an adventure and I've always loved all forms of athletics, so I decided to give it a try. Until then soccer had been my sport and I played it professionally. I had a nasty habit of breaking bones in my leg, however. So I thought perhaps this American job might not be as risky for my body.

It took me a few months to get the hang of place kicking. You can't just stand up there with a strong leg and go to it. Everything must be planned down to the inch. You have 1.3 seconds to get the kick off and if it takes any longer, you're going to have a mouth full of football.

By now you have guessed that I am a soccer-style kicker. Of course there is the conventional style of kicking, that of straight ahead. Both have their advantages and disadvantages. But both require an awful lot of practice and discipline. Both require you to concentrate on a spot. You need good foot-eye coordination. You need a good follow through after you make contact with the ball and you must keep your head down. So there is a lot of mental control in both methods.

A straight ahead, conventional-style kicker uses the toe of his shoe to kick. It is a very effective kick because you get immediate height and so it's difficult to block unless the defense makes excellent penetration. But because of that height, you usually don't get quite the distance you can with a soccer-style kick.

As I see it, the advantages of the soccer-style kick are that, first, more of your foot meets the ball. So there's less chance of hitting it in the wrong place. Also, if the ball isn't set down perfectly on the spot, it is easier to adjust. I can adjust even if the ball is set down six inches off the spot. It's harder to adjust in that situation for a conventional kicker.

So there are advantages and disadvantages to both. There are some outstanding straight ahead kickers in the NFL. But on the whole, the pros prefer the distance that a soccer-style kicker can get more consistently.

That doesn't mean you can go out tomorrow morning and be a soccer-style kicker in two weeks. I think first you need to play a lot of soccer. You need to get used to simply kicking in that manner. There is a tremendous amount of coordination involved in this kick.

One misconception is that you need a strong leg to be a kicker. That's not necessarily true. Soccer-style requires excellent technique. If you don't have that technique, a strong leg won't help much, and with good technique, you can get by without a strong leg. That's because kicking is a lot like swinging a golf club. A conventional-style kicker needs a strong leg because he is not building up the momentum that a soccer-style player does.

With all that in mind let me describe what I do to kick. Remember that there is an awful lot of practice involved in perfecting this. Kicking requires perfect timing and the only way you'll get that timing is by practicing every day.

First, let me explain how I set up. I'll be describing it from the point of view of a left-footed kicker since that's how I kick, but you can transfer it for right-footed by simply reversing what I tell you.

You need to imagine a spot on the ground. In lower levels of ball you are allowed to use a tee, so you don't need to worry much about this. In the pros we're not allowed to use the kicking tee so my spotter puts his finger on the spot on the ground where he wants to set the ball.

From that spot (you can do it from your kicking tee) I line up with my eye a spot two yards inside the left upright. I do this because my kick hooks from left to right and so if I want the ball in the middle of the uprights, I need to allow for that hook. If you're a right-footed kicker, your ball will hook from right to left, so you line up the spot two yards inside the right upright.

From my spot on the ground I take three steps straight back while facing the goal post, beginning with my right foot directly next to the spot. My first step is with the left foot. After these three steps, I take a large step to my right with my right foot. This gives me about a 45° angle with the ball. Because I've done this so many times, I know I am perfectly positioned now for the kick. So I simply concentrate on the spot. My right shoulder and my right foot point to the spot.

On the snap there is a two-step run up before the kick. I step first with my left foot, then make a second, bigger step with my right foot, and when it lands the right foot is next to the spot on the ground and pointing exactly to the spot I'm aiming for between the uprights. All of my momentum now is planted in the right heel. My right leg is bent and flexed.

At this point I twist my hips left to right and thus swing my left foot into the ball. I make contact with the instep of my foot on the lower one-third of the ball. This is very important for height. If you hit the middle of the ball, you'll get a flat kick and risk having it blocked.

When I make contact my leg follows through the middle of the ball. My head stays down and my foot goes as high as it can. The momentum of the kick will lift my right foot off the ground and carry me forward two or three feet. My body will also move a little to the right.

I wear a normal soccer shoe when I kick. I like it very soft with no hard toe. It's just like an ordinary running shoe, except it has soccer cleats. The shoe should be soft enough to give you a good feel of the ball on your instep.

A lot of young kickers are concerned about the rush. You must not worry about it. You should keep your head down and do your job. If you time it right, your kick will not be blocked unless there is a complete breakdown in the blocking. You'd better not worry about that because you only have 1.3 seconds to get the kick off.

A good holder is very important to a kicker. You need to work with him a lot to get your timing. I begin my steps toward the ball as soon as I see him raise his right hand to catch the ball. Though I don't see the ball yet, I know it's on the way. Though it takes a lot of control and concentration, there is still time to adjust if the placement is not on your spot.

The reason I can adjust is because I know my steps exactly. The key is to keep cool and follow through toward the middle of the uprights. Against Detroit once, there was a bad snap from center and the ball was actually laying on the ground. I have a cool holder and he did his best to set up the ball even though I was planted and ready to kick. He didn't actually set it down, it kind of bounced, but I got my foot into the ball and it hit the cross bar and bounced over for a field goal. I feel the reason we made that one was because of concentration and hours of practice.

There isn't too much in the way of adjustment according to field placement and wind. Of course in the pros the hashmarks are close together. So if I'm lined up on the right hashmark, I adjust by changing my target from two yards inside the left upright, to one yard. I do the same on the left hashmark.

If there is a strong wind in my face, I don't change anything. If you try to kick harder you'll mess up your timing and miss the kick. As far as a cross wind you may have to adjust your target some. The pre-game warmup period should help you judge that.

There is absolutely no difference between kicking extra points and kicking field goals. I try to kick every placement the same, with the same rhythm. Sometimes to help on extra points, I practice kicking about six yards away from the goal posts in order to work on my height. But on long field goal attempts I don't try to change that height. Some people think you have to sacrifice some of that height to get more distance. I find that if I get the same height, I get better distance. I think you should try to kick it the same every time. Otherwise you can psyche yourself out on longer kicks.

The most common mistake young kickers make is in the area of concentration. Everyone wants to lift his head and see where the ball is going. However, if you bring your head up too soon, it's like a golf swing where you look up too soon—you top the ball. Your body comes up with your head.

You must work on keeping your head down and keeping it down every time you kick. You must have the same steps, the same approach and the same form in order to become a consistent kicker. I know now exactly where the ball is going when I kick it. I don't have to look up.

It is very important for you to be ready at all times to go in and kick. I strongly suggest you do a lot of flexibility exercises. Do a lot of stretching to keep your muscles loose. If it's cold, I jog up and down the sidelines to keep limber and warm. As soon as our team crosses midfield, I start getting ready. I'm terrified by the thought of not being ready. It hasn't happened to me yet; I've always been ready to go in when they called me. That's very important because eighty percent of kicking, once you've mastered the techniques, is mental.

Just a few words on kickoffs. In order to get distance on soccer-style kickoffs, you need momentum and technique. The last three steps of your approach give you the momentum you need. I always put the ball in the center of the field and line up six yards away on the right hashmark (keep in mind I'm talking about pro ball hashmarks. If you want to use this form, you might line up even with the upright).

I take two slow steps toward the ball and accelerate on the last three steps into the ball. You want to get the exact same follow through that you do on field goals. And you want to hit the bottom third of the football because height is just as important as distance. Your team needs time to get down and cover the kickoff.

People feel there is an awful lot of pressure on a kicker, especially when you have to go in and kick a field goal at the end of the game, one that can make the difference between winning and losing. There is a lot of pressure and there's only one way I've been able to meet it.

When I first made the New England Patriots, I had absolutely no confidence. I really wondered from week to week if I would still be on the team. That's not what you want in a kicker. A kicker needs confidence if he's going to be effective. But I couldn't manufacture it; I really didn't feel I belonged on the team.

There were some teammates of mine who were Christians and they started talking to me about Christ and invited me to their Bible studies each week. I went, but I didn't accept what they said at first. But gradually, I became impressed with the evidence for Christianity.

Before the third regular season game of the 1974 season, we were scheduled to play the Los Angeles Rams, who many people said was the best team in pro football. I was very nervous. I knew the stadium was sold out, and I was worried about missing a field goal and losing the game for our team. I was at my lowest mentally.

At the Bible study that week, all of what I'd been hearing clicked in my mind. I finally said to God, "Look, Jesus, if You really are who they say You are, give me mental strength and use me." At that point I gave up using my own will power and started using His power.

That made a world of difference in my mental outlook. That week we beat LA 20-14 and I kicked two field goals, two extra points and all my kickoffs went into the end zone.

That experience of receiving Christ changed my life, because now it is no longer John Smith trying to make a living, but Jesus Christ living through me. If I feel any pressure on a kick, it's self-inflicted. I don't feel the pressure if I'm thinking of my Lord and playing for Him and meditating on the words He's said in the Bible.

In 1977 we played an exciting overtime game with Cleveland on Monday night television in which I kicked the tying field goal with two seconds left in regulation time. After the game reporters asked me what I was thinking about when I went in. I told them it was Philippians 4:13, a verse in the Bible that says that I can do everything, including kick field goals, through Christ who strengthens me. I wasn't nervous when I went in because I wasn't worrying about the situation, but thinking about God.

I believe that I'm a much better kicker than I would have been had I not become a Christian.

Conditioning
Nate Wright
Minnesota Vikings

Nate Wright started his 10th NFL season in 1978, and his seventh with the Minnesota Vikings. He's been a regular at cornerback for the Vikes since 1974. During his career, which began with the Atlanta Falcons and St. Louis Cardinals, Wright has intercepted 23 passes.

In 1976 he led the Vikings in interceptions with seven. Nate is not considered big for a cornerback, being only 5′11″ tall and weighing 180 pounds, but he makes up for his size with outstanding conditioning and hard work.

If you have any intentions of staying in football for more than a couple of years, you need to start developing an off season training program. You might be able to succeed for a while without conditioning if you're a good athlete. But ultimately, especially if you go past high school, you will pay a price.

Believe it or not, I didn't have a training program until I was already in the pros for a couple of years. I knew I should train, but no one had told me how to train. I did some things right out of ignorance, but my conditioning wasn't set up with any clear cut objectives.

I feel there are four reasons why a football player should train. You've heard most of the players talk about the need for strength. A good training program will provide strength and flexibility. First, that will enhance the longevity of your career. Second, it will help you fulfill your athletic potential. Third, it will help you perform more consistently on the football field. And fourth, it will help prevent injuries.

I would not recommend you start serious training if you are under thirteen years of age. Your body is still growing too much to do the kinds of things I'm recommending. But if you're thirteen or older and you want to be successful in football, I'd recommend you seriously consider what I talk about. Naturally, you should check with your doctor, coach and parents before beginning your program.

There are two basic groupings on a football team for training purposes. One is the skill positions such as quarterback, defensive back, wide receiver, running back and perhaps tight end. The other positions require more size, strength and bulk. The first group requires more skills like catching, running, and jumping. So these two groups have different objectives in training.

My program would be helpful to both groups, but especially to those in the skill positions. My conditioning program involves running. I am not against lifting weights. I would probably be on a weight program of some kind if I had a weight room available near me in the off season.

The skill positions—receivers, offensive and defensive backs—need strength. Linemen and linebackers, in addition, will probably want to build bulk. There are a number of weight training programs to accomplish these objectives and I would recommend you work this out with your coach.

Before I start my workout, no matter what I'm planning to do, I spend time getting loose. This is crucial. It is very important that you warm up properly to minimize the risk of pulled muscles and other injuries. I warm up by first jogging a light 880 or mile. Then I go into a complete flexibility and stretching program.

The flexibility exercises I will describe were given to me by Bob Moore, the athletic trainer at San Diego State University. It is a good routine for warming up before any athletic activity. The purpose of it is to maintain the flexibility of the joints and muscles that are most commonly used in athletics.

There are ten exercises and each should be done five or six times at first, and you should build up to where you

1. *Lateral trunk stretch.* Bend to your right side, sliding your right hand down your leg. Repeat to the left side.

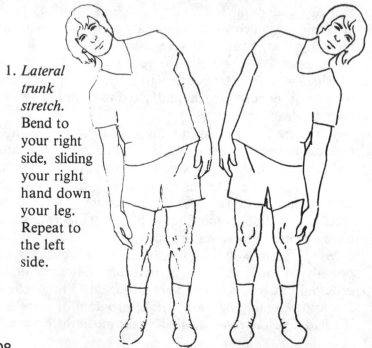

are doing ten repetitions of each exercise. You should repeat them at the end of your workout with four or five
repetitions.

2. *Knee to chest stretch.* Lie on your back and bring
   your right knee as close to your chest and opposite
   shoulder as possible. Then attempt to touch your
   chin to the knee. Alternate by bringing left knee
   toward right shoulder.

3. *Groin stretch.* Get in a sitting position with the soles
   of your feet together, your elbows inside your knees
   and your hands clasped. Push your knees against your
   elbows as hard as you can and hold for two counts.
   Then relax and pull your heels in closer to your crotch
   and repeat.

4. *Hip flexor stretch.* Lying on your stomach, flex one knee at a 90° angle, keeping your knees together. Then raise your thigh off the floor until tightness is felt in front of your hip. Return your thigh to the floor and repeat using your other leg. It is very important to keep your knee bent and tucked toward your inside at all times. Do not hyper-extend your back.

5. *Quadriceps stretch.* In the same position as number four, grasp right ankle with right hand and apply resistance isometrically to knee extension. Hold for two counts, then relax. Bend the knee closer to your hip and repeat. Do the same to your left leg. Remember to keep your knee in line with your shoulder.

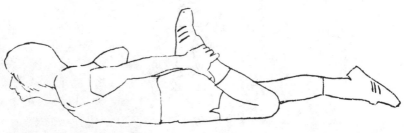

6. *Straight leg raises.* Do one leg at a time, keeping the knee straight. Hold it up until you feel tightness. Keep the opposite leg on the ground and straight.

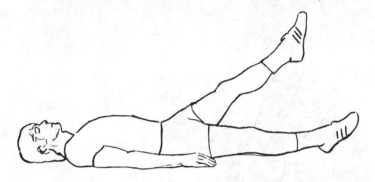

7. *Lower leg extensions.* Lying on your back, keep left leg straight and raise your right thigh to about a 135° angle, holding it with your hands. Straighten the lower half of the leg to the point of tightness.

8. *Calf stretch.* In a standing position lean against a support with both hands. One leg should be behind the other with the heel maintaining contact with the ground. The toe should be slightly turned in and the knees should be straight. Lean slowly forward toward the support by bending the elbows and front leg until tightness is felt in the rear leg. Hold for three counts. Alternate with the other leg.

9. *Anterior ankle stretch.* Use the same position as number eight. Place the top of the toe of your rear foot on the ground with the foot pointed slightly inward. Put gradual pressure down and forward by bending your knees. Hold for three counts and alternate with the other leg.

10. *Ankle stretch.* In standing position, with slight support by your hands, roll to the outside border of your foot, then roll to your inside border.

When you have completed your flexibility exercises, do your skills workout. That is, if you're working on running pass patterns, or throwing passes, or covering receivers, this is the time to do those drills. I usually start working on my skills about a month before training camp but you should start much earlier than that. Because I've played for so many years, it doesn't take me long to sharpen my skills before training camp. The conditioning should come last because when you're done with that, you'll be tired and it won't be a good time to practice skills.

The program I'm giving you is broken into four five-week periods. After the season is over, I usually take about five weeks off to rest my body. Then I begin the following program.

First five weeks: foundational training. This is the foundation for the rest of my training. Three or four times a week, I run long distance, starting with about two miles and working up to eight or 10 miles. The purpose of this is for cardio vascular conditioning. It strengthens your heart, increases your circulation and helps your lungs. This will give you stamina to recover from day to day as you continue the program.

For foundational training, as for the other three programs, you may not be able to do quite as much as I do. If you're just starting, you may want to begin with one mile and work up to four or five miles. You need to be careful not to overtax your body. But as you train, you will be able to build endurance and after doing this for a year or two, you should be able to work at or near these levels.

Second five weeks: strength conditioning. Since I don't work out on weights, I build my strength by running up hills. There is about a 200-yard hill near where I live. I run up it hard four times, with about a five-minute interval in between. I do this three days a week for five weeks, and use a fourth day for distance running to keep up that part of my conditioning.

Third five weeks: interval training. Now I move my training out to the track. I run what we call step downs at half to three quarters speed. I start with a 550, then run in order a 440, 330, 220 and 110. I do this on Monday and Wednesday. On Tuesday and Thursday I run three 330's. Then on Friday I run hills or distance. If I do hills Friday, I'll run distance on Saturday. I want to keep both of these up a little longer though I'll drop them by the time I start my last five-week period.

Final five weeks: sprinting. If you have faithfully followed the first three programs, this fourth program will help build your speed. And as you've read in this book, speed is something that is helpful, if not necessary at every position in football.

Sprinting consists of a series of dashes adding up to 900 yards, which is about the maximum your body can sprint all out in one workout. You can divide these up any way you like, but vary the distances. For example, you might run one 100, two 75's, three 60's, three 50's, five 35's and six 25's. Between each run allow enough time for complete recovery.

I do this workout three times a week, on Monday, Wednesday and Friday. On Tuesday and Thursday, I run five 180 yard dashes.

The advantage of this program is that you're gradually building your body up without putting too much strain on your body at one time. Each program builds on the previous program. I would recommend that you make up a chart several months before your training camp is scheduled to open and map out your program and what you'll be doing specifically each day. Then stick to it. It would help if you have another person to train with. That helps especially on those days when you don't feel like working out. With a partner you can encourage and help each other.

One thing you should not do. Don't start conditioning a week or two before your team opens practice and expect it to do much good. You won't be ready. You need a program and you need a plan for working out most of the off-season.

Two other things to keep in mind. After each workout in this program I've outlined, you'll be very tired. Your body needs rest. Give it that rest. Get plenty of sleep. The other thing is to eat well with good nutrition in mind. I used to take dozens of vitamin pills and other supplements. While these may be helpful, I think ultimately the most important thing is to simply eat well-balanced meals and get the rest you need so the body can build back up after your workouts.

Keep in mind that if you will be faithful in your workouts in the off-season, you'll be a better football player during the season, and as you do this each year, you'll be building speed, strength and endurance. This will help you become a better athlete and thus fulfill your God-given potential. It takes a lot of discipline to be a top athlete and there is no substitute for it.

A Personal Message From the Pros

RAY EASTERLING: As a boy I remember lying on the rug in my grandfather's living room watching the Green Bay Packers on television. I remember watching Paul Hornung and Jim Taylor and thinking, "That's where it's at." I had no idea at that time that I would someday become a professional football player.

But several years later I had the chance to play on the Atlanta Falcons. When I went home after my first NFL season, I had all that I had dreamed of—money, clothes, a car and a certain degree of success. I started participating in the party life, going to different bars, and even tried drugs. At that time in my life, when I had everything I ever wanted, I was so depressed I can remember crying myself to sleep at night.

Right before training camp opened, I read a book called **I Dare You** that talked about being a better person intellectually, socially, physically and spiritually. The author dared you to find out if there was a God and I was the type of person who, if someone dared me to do something, would do it. Well, I found out that God was real, and that His Son Jesus Christ would forgive me of my sins and make me a new person.

BOB BREUNIG: What a thrill it was to win the Super Bowl in 1978. I would like to tell you that winning the Super Bowl was not the highlight of my life, however. Winning the Super Bowl is a temporary experience. Every year there is a new champion and a few years from now, not that many people will care that Dallas won the World Championship in 1978.

The most important event in my life occurred near the end of my senior year at Arizona State University. I had finished a highly successful college career. I'd won many awards. I had a close family, lots of friends and a solid "B" average in school. And yet, something was missing. After all those accomplishments, I was not fulfilled.

About this time two people started talking to me. I learned from them that everyone has a problem called sin. Sin is man living independently from God, and its evidence is demonstrated in many ways, both large and small. The Bible says that the penalty for sin is death (spiritual separation from God; see Romans 6:23). But God provided an escape in the person of Jesus Christ, God's son. I didn't accept this right away but the more I thought about it, the more it made sense. Finally in the spring of 1975, I allowed Christ to come into my life, to forgive me of my sins and take over control of my life.

JIM ZORN: In high school I found that there wasn't much wrong with my life. I had many friends and things were going great. And I thought I was a Christian. I believed in God and in Jesus Christ. After all—I was born in America. But when my girlfriend invited me to go to a Campus Life meeting, I learned I was wrong about Christianity.

I found out that a Christian was not just a person who was born in America or who lived a good life. Being a

Christian is knowing Christ as your personal Savior. This started a struggle in my life. I thought if I became a Christian, I'd have to give up football and girls and become religious. The more I learned, especially as I read the Bible, the more I realized that I didn't have to change. Any changes that needed to be made in my life, God would make.

So I did pray and receive Christ. And God didn't send me to Africa. He didn't make me quit liking football. I didn't have to quit liking girls. What was exciting was that I felt like I was a new person.

CHARLIE SANDERS: I was never a bad kid and I always felt there was a God, a Superior Being. But I didn't know how to reach Him. At a chapel service for the Lions, I learned that you have to invite Jesus Christ into your life.

I finally did that in the dugout in Cleveland as we were waiting to go out and play the Browns. I asked Jesus Christ to forgive me of my sins and to take control of my life. He did, just as He promised He would in the Bible. One of the biggest changes He's made is that I no longer worry. I place everything in His hands.

MIKE McCOY: It was a tremendous honor to be drafted second among all the football players in the country by the Green Bay Packers. They had a great tradition and when I joined the team, they still had many players left from those great championship seasons of the 1960's.

Two of those players had a great impact on my life. One was Carroll Dale, a great wide receiver. One day I asked Carroll what it was that made him different. He told me that he was a Christian and had dedicated his life to Jesus Christ.

Through Carroll I started attending the chapel services our team held before every game. These programs are now a part of every football team in the NFL. I listened to the speakers and asked questions. I learned that there is a difference between Christianity and religion. Religion is man's effort to reach God. Christianity is God reaching down to man in the person of Jesus Christ.

JEFF SIEMON: It took a serious knee injury to bring me to Christ. My career almost ended before it began during my freshman year at Stanford when I tore three of the four ligaments in my knee.

Soon after my injury I received a letter from a hometown friend who told me that she experienced a relationship with Jesus Christ and that Christ was exactly what was needed in my life. The day after I received this letter, there was a visitor to my room and he was talking to my roommate about Jesus Christ. So I confronted him and asked him how one came into a personal relationship with Christ. He told me that it was simply a matter of believing that I was separated from God, believing Jesus could heal that separation and then asking Him to come into my life.

I waited until this visitor and my roommate had left, then bowed my head and talked with Christ. I said, "Jesus, I don't know what in the world You have planned for my life, but I know that on my own I have failed. I ask You to come into my life and change it according to Your will."

JOHN SMITH: I was proud of being an intellectual person and therefore thought the Bible was a bunch of myths. I thought Jesus Christ was a religious teacher like Buddha. Even though I'd gone to church most of my life, I didn't really understand that Jesus Christ was God and that the Bible was truth, not myth.

A number of people started giving me books to read, such as **The Late Great Planet Earth.** I was impressed that everything about Christ was predicted hundreds of years before He was born. It was too much to be a coincidence. These facts, coupled with my need for confidence in my life, caused me to accept Christ into my life. Christ has changed my whole outlook on life.

JOHN HANNAH: It is quite a thrill to be named the outstanding offensive lineman in the National Football League. But I must be honest with you, the honors I have received in football don't have nearly the meaning that knowing Jesus Christ does.

I became a Christian—that is I received Christ as my Savior—when I was nine years old. As I grew older other things became more important, particularly football. I began to think of Jesus Christ as a Santa Claus—someone you only believed in when you were a kid.

That attitude caused a lot of problems because I made a mess out of my life, despite being very successful on the football field. For example, my wife and I were separated for six months. When we got back together, she was a different person because she had committed her life to Christ. Through her I realized I needed to make a decision, and I asked Christ to retake control of my life.

The moment I did that, I knew I had complete forgiveness of my sins, and I began seeing some changes in my life. I'm still not the person I want to be or should be, but I can see myself changing for the better through Christ.

BARNEY CHAVOUS: I came from a very good family, and at the age of thirteen I accepted Christ into my life. I knew I had something in my life at that point, but I didn't know what. Then in college I started getting into the Bible and it told me what had happened, and I started to grow spiritually.

I've continued to grow through my career in pro ball because there are a number of Christians on the Denver Broncos. We get together frequently to study the Bible, encourage each other and pray for each other. The Christian life is a lot like growing up as a person. You start out as a little baby. Soon you are crawling. Then you try to get up and you fall down, but after a while you start walking. A few more months and you start running. After years and years, some people end up running a marathon; they can't do that the moment they're born. It's the same way as far as growing in the Christian life.

DUANE CARRELL: I became a Christian while I was playing with the Dallas Cowboys. A number of teammates invited me to their Bible study, but I had a hard time accepting what they said. After the season was over, I decided to read the New Testament to find out what was the truth. As I did, it hit me that it was true and that Christ was my Savior.

There are no doubt other kickers with more talent than me who haven't had a chance to play pro ball like I have. I could be disappointed that I didn't play better than I did, but I thank God that I've had the opportunity. Through football I've met Christ, which is the most important decision I will ever make in my entire life.

RICH SAUL: I knew about Christ when I was a kid, but there is a difference between knowing about Christ and being a committed Christian. To be totally committed as a Christian, you have to walk with Christ every day. You have to let the Holy Spirit guide you and read the Bible for instruction.

That allows you to have a great day every day based on your attitude. I see it a little like a relationship with our parents. If the only time we went to our parents was to ask them for something, it would not be the same as if we sometimes just went up and said we love them and spent some time with them. God wants us to enjoy Him, not to just go to Him with our problems.

ROBERT MILLER: My purpose for playing pro football is to glorify Jesus Christ and help spread His good news. In the Bible (Philippians 4:13) it says, "I can do all things through Him (Christ) who strengthens me." That means a lot to me.

It's easy to praise God when things go well, but if I fumble or drop a pass, I still praise God. This verse in the Bible reminds me that I can. I've learned that every situation, whether good or bad, can bring me closer to God, so I thank Him and praise Him whether something goes well or not.

ARCHIE GRIFFIN: I grew up in a Christian home and my parents' number one priority was Christ. One thing that impressed me was that while we didn't have a lot, you didn't notice it because our home was full of joy. So when I was in eighth grade, I accepted Christ.

My priorities are as follows: being a Christian is number one, then my family, then my education and finally football. Sometimes it's hard to keep that balance. In high school, while I still thought Christ was important, I pushed Him back because no one else was talking about Him. But that was wrong. Now I try to keep Christ number one in my life, where He belongs.

GEORGE BUEHLER: The number one thing that impresses me about being a Christian is that I am of tremendous value. God loves me for who I am. God loves me no matter what I do because of the payment His Son Jesus Christ made for my sins. Because He loves me so much, it makes me love God and want to please Him.

Many people try to condense Christianity into a list of rules and regulations. But the Bible says I am free to live without all of the restrictions of religious laws. The difference is that now I read the Bible and learn what God wants for me. Because of His love for me, I respond by trying to do what He wants me to do.

STEVE LARGENT: When I play football, I play for an audience of one. God gave me a certain amount of ability to play football, and to honor Him, I need to use that ability to the maximum. My incentive is to play to 100% of *my* God-given talents. I never try to be as good as someone else. If I play to my best, I am a winner in God's eyes no matter what the final score is.

There is a comparison from football that helps me understand my own Christian life. If I don't concentrate on the football in a game, I will have a tough time catching the passes thrown in my direction. I've found the same is true in my Christian walk. When I fail to concentrate daily on Christ, it seems incomplete.

BRAD COUSINO: Becoming a Christian wasn't a big emotional experience for me. In fact, for a while, I wondered if anything had really happened. But within a few weeks, I began to see some changes in my life, such as my wanting to read the Bible. For example, I had a bad temper—little things could easily make me blow up.

One day I walked out of my apartment and noticed that someone had stolen my car stereo tapes, worth about $250. Based on previous responses I should have been furious, but I only thought, "I hope the guy enjoys those tapes." That response surprised me.

Another area of change was my language. I was always swearing and taking the Lord's name in vain. Now, I rarely do. My temperament has changed and I am able to relax and enjoy life more. I feel happy inside!

CRAIG MORTON: I was introduced to Jesus Christ by my wife, Susie. I had always felt a need in my life, but I rejected Christianity. I didn't want to make the sacrifice. I never opened my heart and said to the Lord, "Here is my life." I finally did that in 1977.

There is a verse in the Bible (Romans 10:9) that sums up what I believe: "If you confess with your mouth Jesus as Lord, and believe in your heart that God raised Him from the dead, you shall be saved."

To me that means if I really believe Jesus Christ is my Savior, I need to talk about it and tell others. That's why I spoke out in 1977 when members of the press asked me what had changed my life. If Christ loves me enough to die for me, then it certainly isn't asking too much for me to speak for Him when I have the opportunity.

JEAN BARRETT: My life is living proof of the miracles that Jesus Christ can perform when one asks Him to come into one's life and take control. Where once there was no purpose, now there is the purpose of serving Him; where there was once only the satisfaction of natural desires and material goals, now there is a satisfied mind at peace with God. This change came as the result of the need for Jesus Christ in my life.

My Christian growth has been a slow process. Every day I try to turn over more of my life to Him. Prayer has become a very important part of my life, and every year I am made more aware of how God truly answers our prayers.

NATE WRIGHT: The main reason I became a Christian is that once you understand Scripture and see that Jesus is who He says He is—the Son of God—you have to respond. I enjoy the wisdom and knowledge that I get from being a Christian. I can now understand why things happen on earth and in society. I have a better understanding of people in general. It used to puzzle me why there was corruption, stealing, greed, selfishness. Now I see that it is simply man's basic nature when he is separated from God. Only God can change these things in the life of a man.

MIKE FULLER: Today people are looking for something to turn to, something to give them the right motivation and attitude toward life. There are so many things to turn to—transcendental meditation, various cults, drugs, sex, etc. People are searching for anything that will give them peace, something they can rely on.

I have found from personal experience that Christ is the only One we can truly rely on. Christianity is the only faith that is based on a living, risen Savior. No one who has given Jesus Christ a real, honest try has ever ruined his life. Christ has only made it better. I believe that the Christian life is the best life to live. There is no comparison to knowing the living God personally.

Putting It All Together
Norm Evans
Seattle Seahawks

The pro football career of Norm Evans began in 1965 and has included numerous honors. He played in three Super Bowls and on two Super Bowl champion teams with the Miami Dolphins. He was the last of the original Dolphins drafted in the expansion pool of 1966. He was a starter at offensive tackle for ten straight seasons and appeared in a club record 138 games. Twice he was voted the team's outstanding offensive lineman and he played in the 1973 and 1975 Pro Bowls.

In 1976 Norm was again a member of an expansion team, being picked by Seattle in the veteran allocation. He quickly proved his worth on the young team, being named co-captain each of the first three seasons. He was part of an offensive line that was fourth in NFL pass protection the first two seasons, allowing only 49 sacks. He was the first Seahawk player to be inducted into the Kingdome Hall of Fame. And he was the Seahawk fans' nominee for Seattle Sports Star of the Year.

Norm stands 6′ 5″ and weighs 250 pounds. He was drafted out of Texas Christian by Houston in 1964, and made the starting team his rookie season. He has authored two books about his football experiences: **On God's Squad** and **On the Line.** He is also president of Pro Athletics Outreach, a Christian ministry for professional athletes.

I have had many great experiences in professional football. I can still remember the day I was drafted in 1964. I really didn't expect to be picked, but I was reading the newspaper, looking down the list of guys I'd played with and against who were being drafted in the National and American Football Leagues. Then a name jumped out at me and I got so excited I was jumping up and down. "I've been drafted by the Oilers!", I yelled as my wife came running into the living room. She didn't understand though; she thought I was going to work for a gas station.

That day is still vivid in my mind because I'd always dreamed of having a chance to play pro ball. But as exciting as that was, it wasn't the most important or meaningful experience of my life.

There was the day when the Miami Dolphins made the playoffs for the first time, achieving their first winning season in the process, and I was voted the team's unsung hero. What a thrill that was, after experienceing the frustration of several losing seasons, to be recognized as being an important part of the team's new success. But that wasn't the greatest experience of my life.

Two years later, we achieved the ultimate in professional football. The Miami Dolphins went through the entire regular season and playoffs undefeated and untied. We won the Super Bowl over Washington to become the only modern pro team to complete a perfect 17-0 season. It was a thrill to be a starter on what will be considered one of the great teams in professional football history. But that wasn't the greatest experience of my life.

That season I achieved another dream of mine— I was voted by my peers to play for the AFC in the Pro Bowl Game. Not only was I playing for the best football team in America, but I was playing in the game that included only the best individuals at each position. That meant a lot, too, but it wasn't the greatest experience of my life.

I could go on. There was another Super Bowl championship; another Pro Bowl appearance. There were honors such as team captain with the Seattle Seahawks. But none of them compare with the greatest experience of my life.

That came back in 1966 as I was in training camp, preparing for my first season with the Miami Dolphins. My wife, Bobbie, and I went to hear a man speak, and he told about how a person could become a Christian.

I really thought I was a Christian before then. I went to church occasionally and I was a good person. But this speaker pointed out that going to church and being a good person weren't even the issues. The problem was two-fold. First every single person, including Norm Evans, falls short of God's standard of perfection. Second, I had never accepted Jesus for who He said He was.

For the first time I really learned who Jesus Christ is. He is God. He came and lived on this earth in human flesh. He lived the perfect life, and then was brutally killed, in order to pay the penalty for my sin. Jesus Christ was God's only Son, and yet the Father was willing to give Him up, to let Him die a horrible death for my sins, and for the sins of the whole world. And He would have done it just for me even if I was the only person in the world.

That really gets to me. I have a son named Ronnie. Much as I might love you—and I do love you—there is no way I'd be willing to have my son die for you or for anyone. I couldn't bear to do that. And yet, that's how much God loves me, that He was willing to let His only son die for me.

However, Jesus Christ didn't stay dead. Three days after His death, He came back to life, and by doing so, He allows me and everyone who wants to, to know Him personally. The Bible says, "To as many as received Him, to them He gave the right to become children of God" (John 1:12).

What does it mean to receive Christ? I remember vividly one play in Super Bowl X, probably one of the most exciting of the Super Bowl games played to date. The game was very close in the fourth quarter when Terry Bradshaw of the Steelers dropped back to pass. Lynn Swann flew down the field and broke into the open on a post pattern.

Bradshaw lofted a beautiful pass toward Swann. Running at full speed Swann took the ball over his shoulder—he received the pass—and kept running for the touchdown, a 64-yard play that broke the backs of the Dallas Cowboys. As he crossed the goal line, the referee's arms shot up, six points went on the scoreboard and 78,000 fans jumped up and roared. That play will always be a great memory in Super Bowl history.

But suppose, instead of catching that ball, Lynn Swann had run down the field and as the ball arrived, he had kept his hands down and not received the pass. The referee would have waved his arms ruling an incomplete pass; the 78,000 fans would have groaned in disappointment; no points would have gone up on the scoreboard and the Pittsburgh Steelers might have well lost their momentum and ended up losing the championship. It certainly wouldn't have been remembered as one of the great plays in Super Bowl history.

What was the difference? Lynn Swann put his hands out and received the pass. And that's exactly what we must do to become Christians. We must receive Jesus Christ, we must reach out and take Him into our lives. He doesn't force Himself on us. We have a choice. We can either receive Him or reject Him.

Each of the men who told you how to play football in this book have made personal commitments to Jesus Christ. They have received Him into their lives. While each player is an expert in his area of professional football, he realizes that knowing how to play football isn't enough for living a satisfactory life.

Too many men learn late that the goal of playing professional football and making a big contract isn't the ultimate in life. It isn't the most important thing you can do. It's true that, if you have the ability and work hard enough, you can play pro football. And if you're fortunate enough not to be seriously injured, you can play for several years. I've been fortunate to play fourteen years. Nothing you ever accomplish in football, though, can match the importance of knowing Jesus Christ. He is the One who can give you forgiveness of sin, and therefore allow you to experience eternal life with God.

If you have never accepted Christ into your life, I'd like to give you an opportunity right now. Receiving Christ is an act of your will. God knows your heart. But I would like to give you a simple prayer that will help you realize that, at this moment, Christ will come into your life if you ask Him. He promised to do just that in Revelation 3:20: "Behold, I stand at the door (of your life) and knock; if anyone hears My voice and opens the door, I will come in to him."

If this prayer expresses your desire, pray it as you read: "Lord Jesus, I need You. I open the door of my life and invite You in. Please forgive me of my sins. Thank You for dying on the cross for me. Please make me the kind of person You want me to be."

If you prayed that prayer and really meant it, Jesus Christ is in your life right now and you have eternal life with Him. If you have never asked Christ to come into your life and forgive you of your sins, I'd like for you to consider what Jesus Christ said in the Bible (in John 3:36): "He who believes in the Son (Jesus Christ) has eternal life; but he who does not obey the Son shall not see life, but the wrath of God abides on him" (NIV).

So you have two choices. You can either receive Him, or you can reject Him. You should consider the consequences if you reject Him.

The choice is up to you.

If you are interested in what these football players had to say about the Christian life and would like to know more about either how to become a Christian, or what to do after asking Christ into your life, write to:

PRO ATHLETES OUTREACH
P.O. Box 15736
Phoenix, AZ 85060

Notes

The Offense

TACKLE	GUARD	CENTER	GUARD	TACKLE	TIGHT END
O	O	O	O	O	O
Jean Barrett San Francisco 49ers	George Buehler Cleveland Browns	Rich Saul Los Angeles Rams	John Hannah New England Patriots		Charlie Sanders Detroit Lions

WIDE RECEIVER

O

Steve Largent
Seattle Seahawks

QUARTERBACK

Craig Morton, Denver Broncos
Jim Zorn, Seattle Seahawks

RUNNING BACKS

O   O   O

Archie Griffin, Cincinnati Bengals
Robert Miller, Minnesota Vikings

The Defense

END

☐

Barney Chavous
Denver Broncos

TACKLE

☐

TACKLE

☐

Mike McCoy
Oakland Raiders

END

☐

LINEBACKERS

☐

☐

☐

Bob Breunig
Dallas Cowboys

Jeff Siemon
Minnesota Vikings

Brad Cousino
Toronto Argonauts

☐

☐

BACKS

☐

☐

Ray Easterling
Atlanta Falcons